WWW Motivation Mining:

Finding Treasures for Teaching Evaluation Skills Grades 7-12

**Ruth V. Small
and
Marilyn P. Arnone**

PROFESSIONAL GROWTH SERIES®

A Publication of THE BOOK REPORT & LIBRARY TALK
Professional Growth Series

Linworth Publishing, Inc.
Worthington, Ohio

This book is dedicated to
our beloved parents:
Ella and Myron Small (in loving memory)
Gladys and Len Mathieu

Library of Congress Cataloging-in-Publication Data

Published by Linworth Publishing, Inc.
480 East Wilson Bridge Road, Suite L
Worthington, Ohio 43085

Copyright©1999 by Linworth Publishing, Inc.

Series Information:
    From The Professional Growth Series

All rights reserved. Reproduction of this book in whole or in part is prohibited without permission of the publisher.

some images copyright www.arttoday.com

ISBN 0-938865-89-7

5 4 3 2 1

Acknowledgements

We wish to acknowledge the outstanding dedication and commitment of the researchers, teachers, and library media specialists who contributed so much to the writing of this book. Their stories relating their efforts to improve the information literacy of their students were nothing less than inspiring. We also wish to express our gratitude to the students at the School of Information Studies at Syracuse University who provided us with critical feedback during the development of the *WebMAC* instruments. Special thanks to Mike Eisenberg for writing the foreword to this book and to the folks at Linworth Publishing, Inc., for their encouragement and support as we prepared this manuscript. Last but not least, we acknowledge the following friends and relatives who, long before this book was ever written, provided loving support and encouragement: Joan and Rosamond Adler, Sonja and Glenn Cooper, Hannah Joseph, and Gayle Kadlik.

Author Biographies

Ruth V. Small, Ph.D., is Associate Professor and Director of the School Media Program at the School of Information Studies at Syracuse University. She holds a master's degree in education from Hunter College in New York City, and a master's degree in library science from Syracuse University in Syracuse, New York where she received her doctorate in instructional design, development, and evaluation. Ruth's teaching and research focus on applying motivation theories to a variety of information-based learning, work, and virtual environments. "Dr. Ruth," as she is affectionately known by her students, was voted 1996 "Professor of the Year" by graduate students of her school at Syracuse. In 1997 she was awarded the AASL/Highsmith Research Award for her innovative research on the motivational strategies used by library media specialists when teaching information skills to students. She is a national and international consultant and speaker on motivation and evaluation.

Marilyn P. Arnone, Ph.D., is a children's media consultant and producer who loves working with children. She has a unique interdisciplinary background, blending practical experience and an understanding of electronic and broadcast media with strong credentials in education. Marilyn is President, New Product Research and Development, of Creative Media Solutions, Inc., where her adventures have covered the gamut from researching and writing educational videos and multimedia for government and corporate clients to conducting a comprehensive formative evaluation for a nationally televised children's program. Her research interests have centered on exploring children's motivation and learning in interactive multimedia environments. Marilyn received her master's degree in education from Harvard University and her doctorate in instructional design, development, and evaluation from Syracuse University.

Foreword

When Ruth Small and Marilyn Arnone asked me to write the foreword for this book, I was pleased to do so because I consider both Ruth and Marilyn good friends and colleagues. And frankly, I would have made some positive and flattering comments even if the book was just "okay." Marilyn and Ruth are two of the most creative people I know, and I would have been able to stress my personal experiences of working with both of them on research, teaching, and creative projects.

I think back to all the collaborative curriculum and program planning that I've done with Ruth at the School of Information Studies at Syracuse University as well as our joint "information-based education" research and work on the Gateway to Educational Materials (GEM) project. With Marilyn, I remember the energy and excitement of working on a video for the Educational Resources Information Center (ERIC)—particularly her "surprise" version—a *Star Wars* takeoff that perfectly communicated our message of a new, cutting-edge ERIC.

However, there's no need to dwell on past accomplishments because this new venture is highly impressive on its own. THIS IS IMPORTANT WORK!!

Today, our information-intensive world is fundamentally different than it was just five years ago. The World Wide Web has completely changed the way people of all ages find and use information. We truly are overloaded with information. That's why everyone agrees that students must learn to be discriminating users of information. It's not enough for students to simply find information. They must know that there are varying degrees of quality, and they must be skilled in evaluating information quality through the application of criteria.

And, while lots of people (including me) talked about the need to help students develop these essential skills, Marilyn and Ruth went ahead and did something about it. They created a complete approach—"Motivation Mining"—to help students learn to "mine" quality information on the Web. Based on sound theory, Motivation Mining offers practical and easy-to-use techniques and tools for students and teachers. The heart of the approach is a flexible tool called *WebMac*, the *Web Site Motivational Analysis Checklist*, with versions for teachers and students at different levels. *WebMac* can be used for teaching, lesson-planning, and classroom-based research. But enough of me trying to explain Motivation Mining—Marilyn and Ruth do a far better job throughout this well-planned and well-executed book.

Evaluating information is central to every part of the information problem-solving process. For example, every stage in the Big6 process requires students to be able to evaluate information: in defining the key elements of an information problem, deciding on an information seeking strategy, selecting keywords to locate sources, identifying relevant information in sources, combining information in a product, and evaluating effectiveness and efficiency. With Motivation Mining, we finally have direction and substance in how to go about helping students to learn these essential evaluation abilities. Well done, and thanks, Marilyn and Ruth!

Mike Eisenberg
Seattle, Washington

Table of Contents

DEDICATION
ACKNOWLEDGEMENTS i
AUTHOR BIOGRAPHIES ii
FOREWORD iii
PREFACE x
    Purpose & Intended Audience xi
    Organization of This Book xi

PART I: MOTIVATION MINING FOR INFORMATION LITERACY 1

Chapter One: Evaluation As A Critical Information Skill
    MineMap 3
    Introduction 4
    Objectives 4
    Information Literacy 4
    Evaluation as an Information Skill 5
    Evaluating Information Resources 6
    Web Sites as Information Resources in Education 6
    Web Resources for Teaching and Learning 7
    Evaluating Web Resources 9
    Coming Up 11
    Endnotes 11
    Highlights of Chapter One 13
    Minestorming 14

Chapter Two: Motivation Mining and the World Wide Web
    MineMap 15
    Introduction 16
    Objectives 16
    Motivation and Learning 16
    E-V Theory in the Classroom 17
    E-V Theory in Electronic Environments 18
    Motivation Mining: What Is It, and Why Is It Important? 19
    Teacher Judgments of Content Validity 19
    Students' Perceptions of Motivational Quality 20
    A Web Site's Motivational Attributes: The Pivotal Factor 21
    Web Sites That Have What It Takes 24
    Putting It All Together 25
    Coming Up 26

Table of Contents continued

    Endnotes 26
    Highlights of Chapter Two 27
    Minestorming 28

PART II: MINING TOOLS FOR MOTIVATIONAL ASSESSMENT 29

Chapter Three: Using a Motivational Assessment Tool to Evaluate Web Resources

    Mine Map 31
    Introduction 32
    Objectives 32
    Existing Web Evaluation Instruments 32
    The *Website Motivational Analysis Checklist* 34
    WebMAC Senior 35
    Other *WebMAC* Instruments 35
    Development and Testing 37
    Three Ways To Use Web Site Motivational Assessment 38
        A Teaching Tool 38
        A Lesson-Planning Tool 39
        A Research and Design Tool 39
    Coming Up 41
    Endnotes 41
    Highlights of Chapter Three 41
    Minestorming 42

Chapter Four: Administering the Instrument

    MineMap 43
    Introduction 44
    Objectives 44
    Why Evaluation? 44
    Defining Common Terms 44
    Providing an Overview 45
    Interacting with the Web Site 45
    Giving Students Directions 46
    You As the Model 46
    Ours Is Not the Only Way 46
    Coming Up 48
    Highlights of Chapter Four 48
    Minestorming 49

Table of Contents continued

Chapter Five: *WebMAC Senior*
- MineMap 51
- Introduction 52
- Objectives 52
- Using *WebMAC Senior* with High School Students 52
- *WebMAC Motivational Analysis Checklist: WebMAC Senior* (4.0) 53
- Coming Up 56
- Highlights of Chapter Five 56
- Minestorming 57

Chapter Six: Scoring the Instrument
- MineMap 59
- Introduction 60
- Objectives 60
- Scoring *WebMAC Senior* 60
- Transforming Scores 61
- Plotting the Scores 62
- Rating the Web Site (Individual) 63
- Class Tally 64
- Rating the Web Site (Class) 65
- Coming Up 66
- Highlights of Chapter Six 66
- Minestorming 67

Chapter Seven: Interpreting Results
- MineMap 69
- Introduction 70
- Objectives 70
- Interpreting Scores for the Four Attributes 70
- Pinpointing Trouble Spots 71
- Explaining the Significance of the V and XS Scores 72
- Interpreting Your Overall Motivational Quality Rating 72
- Awesome Web Sites 74
- Coming Up 76
- Highlights of Chapter Seven 76
- Minestorming 77

Table of Contents continued

PART III: PANNING FOR WEB GOLD: MAKING MOTIVATION MINING WORK FOR YOU 79

Chapter Eight: A Treasure Trove of Ideas From Educators
    MineMap 81
    Introduction 82
    Objectives 82
    Gems and Nuggets from the "MasterMines" 82
    Coming Up 93
    Endnotes 93
    Highlights of Chapter Eight 93
    Minestorming 94

Chapter Nine: Other Great Ideas for Using *WebMAC Senior*
    MineMap 95
    Introduction 96
    Objectives 96
    More Gems and Nuggets from the "MasterMines" 96
    WebMAC Senior for Lesson-Planning 96
    WebMAC Senior for Research and Design 99
    Coming Up 105
    Endnotes 105
    Highlights of Chapter Nine 105
    Minestorming 106

Chapter Ten: Motivation Mining into the Future
    MineMap 107
    Introduction 108
    Objectives 108
    Information Skills for the 21st Century 108
    Final Thoughts 109
    Coming Up 110
    Endnotes 110
    Highlights of Chapter Ten 110
    Minestorming 111

Table of Contents continued

PART IV: SHARING THE WEALTH 113

Chapter Eleven: A Workshop for Educators
    MineMap 115
    Introduction 116
    Objectives 116
    Materials 116
    Workshop Outline 116
    Overhead Transparency Masters 118
    Handouts 137
    Coming Up 142
    Highlights of Chapter Eleven 142
    Minestorming 143

Chapter Twelve: Teaching Students to Use *WebMAC Senior*
    MineMap 145
    Introduction 146
    Objectives 146
    Materials 146
    Outline for Integrating Overheads 146
    Overhead Transparency Masters 148
    The "Awsome Website" Award (*AW*Ard) 162
    Highlights of Chapter Twelve 163
    Minestorming 164

BIBLIOGRAPHY 166
APPENDICES 167
    Appendix A: Lesson Plans 169
    Appendix B: *WebMAC Middle* Instrument, Scoring Sheets,
        Class Tally, & Plotting Grids 173
    Appendix C: Content Validity Checklist 183
INDEX 187

Preface

Do your students have that glassy-eyed look from spending hours on the World Wide Web, searching for information or just plain surfing? Today's students are swept up in a "virtual gold rush" on the Web, much like many 19th century Americans during the California Gold Rush. As they dig for Web "gems" to help with homework assignments or just to satisfy their curiosity, the number of Web sites they must wade through quickly turns their "information mother lode" into a bad case of "information overload."

As today's students prepare to be information literate citizens for the 21st century, we need to help them learn to critically evaluate the wide range of information resources they will encounter. As students use the Web more and more for everything from research to browsing just for fun, they will need to acquire the skills and learn to use tools for "motivation mining" the Web and distinguishing Web "gold" from worthless pyrite (better known as "fool's gold").

We begin with a definition of *Motivation Mining* (although it will be defined again later in the book). We define "motivation mining the Web" as the identification and extraction of Web resources that have the potential to enhance student learning by meeting important motivational criteria. Those motivational criteria are at the heart of this book.

Purpose & Intended Audience

The purpose of this book is to describe an innovative Web evaluation tool developed specifically for use by high school students and designed to provide hands-on experience in critically evaluating the strengths and weaknesses of World Wide Web sites. But this book is much more than just a Web evaluation instrument. It places Web evaluation into the larger context of information literacy and provides concrete examples (from us and many of your colleagues) of how to use Web evaluation with students. This affirms the philosophy that one of the best ways to learn is from the experience of others. We share real-life stories from middle and high school educators, who offer practical, easy-to-use ways of applying motivational assessment techniques to the Web site selection process and provide insight into successful strategies that can be used in conjunction with Web-based projects and assignments.

The intended audience for this book includes classroom teachers, library media specialists, and others who work with middle or high school students to develop and improve their information literacy skills. The ideas and examples in this book were chosen specifically for this audience.*

This book should also be useful to teachers and other educators who are involved in or are planning to design a Web site or conduct practical research on effectiveness of Web sites. It includes practical tips, teaching testimonials, lesson plans, and examples of incorporating motivation into teaching, learning, and research experiences using the Web.

Organization of This Book

This book uses a workbook format and is organized into four major parts. Each part contains several chapters, briefly described below. At the end of each chapter, we provide "Chapter Highlights" (a review of key points) and a "Minestorming" (individual brainstorming, with a "mining twist") page for the reader to record any original thoughts and ideas stimulated by reading that chapter. Because this book is based on our concept of "motivation mining," we carry a mining theme throughout the book.

Part I: Motivation Mining for Information Literacy defines the term "motivation mining" and focuses on the relationships among information literacy, motivation, and the evaluation of Web resources. Part I contains the following chapters:

---

* *Our companion book, "WWW Motivation Mining: Finding Treasures for Teaching Evaluation Skills (Grades 1-6)," parallels the motivation theories and concepts presented in this book. Its examples, applications, teacher workshop, and student lessons target elementary educators.*

Chapter One: Evaluation as a Critical Information Skill reviews evaluation as part of a larger information literacy context, describes the variety of educational resources and services available on the Internet and the challenge of evaluating them, and discusses the shortcomings of existing methods for Web site evaluation.

Chapter Two: Motivation Mining and the World Wide Web discusses motivation and its importance in evaluation and introduces the concept of *motivation mining*. It describes the concept of *motivational quality* and discusses the issues of content and validity, as well as functionality, framing them in terms of their effect on motivation. A simple formula for successful Web sites is introduced.

Part II: Mining Tools for Motivational Assessment describes some existing Web evaluation tools and includes *WebMAC Senior©**, an evaluation instrument that focuses on the motivational quality of Web sites, designed for grade 9 through adult. Complete administration directions and scoring forms are also provided. Part II contains the following chapters:

Chapter Three: Using a Motivational Assessment Tool to Evaluate Web Resources introduces the theoretical foundation for the *WebMAC Senior* motivational assessment tool. This chapter describes how *WebMAC Senior* differs from other Web evaluation instruments, discusses the development and testing of the instrument, and explains the variety of ways to use the tool.

Chapter Four: Administering the Instrument provides specific directions for using *WebMAC Senior* with students.

Chapter Five: WebMAC Senior presents the reproducible instrument.

Chapter Six: Scoring the Instrument provides detailed directions for scoring *WebMAC Senior* (version 4.0), including individual and class tally sheets, a scoring key for transforming scores as well as graphs and grids for visually representing scoring results.

Chapter Seven: Interpreting Results discusses how to help students understand what their scores mean and how their evaluation results may be used to revise and improve Web sites.

Part III: Panning for Web Gold: Making Motivation Mining Work for You provides a plethora of ideas, lesson plans, and examples (submitted by classroom teachers and library media specialists) for using and integrating *WebMAC Senior* into the secondary curriculum. Additional ideas from the authors are included. Part III contains the following chapters:

Chapter Eight: A Treasure Trove of Ideas from Educators includes stories from middle and high school practitioners relating how they are using *WebMAC Senior* (and *WebMAC Middle©***) to teach evaluation

---

*copyright, R.V. Small and M.P. Arnone, 1999.
**copyright, R.V. Small and M.P. Arnone, 1999.

skills to their students. The educators provide insight into successful motivational strategies that they have applied to projects and assignments.

Chapter Nine: Other Great Ideas for Using WebMAC Senior describes ways to use *WebMAC Senior* for planning lessons, conducting educational research, and designing new Web sites.

Chapter Ten: Motivation Mining into the Future provides our final thoughts on *motivation mining* for developing information literate citizens for the 21st century.

Part IV: Sharing the Wealth provides materials for offering inservice professional workshops and lessons for students. Part IV contains the following chapters:

Chapter Eleven: A Workshop for Educators includes a workshop outline, reproducible overhead masters and handouts, and a certificate of achievement for teaching your colleagues how to use *WebMAC Senior* (or *WebMAC Middle*) with their students.

Chapter Twelve: Teaching Students to Use WebMAC Senior includes reproducible overhead masters and accompanying content outline to incorporate into a lesson on Web evaluation.

Appendices

▶ *Appendix A: **Lesson Plans*** provides the actual plans used to teach two of the lessons described in Chapter Eight.

▶ ***Appendix B:** WebMAC Middle* includes the reproducible *WebMAC Middle* instrument, tally sheets and scoring grids, designed for use by students in Grades 5-8 but also appropriate for use as a shorter and simpler form of *WebMAC Senior*.

PART I

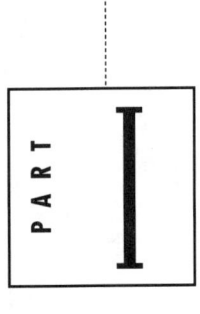

Motivation Mining For Information Literacy

CHAPTER 1

Evaluation As a Critical Information Skill

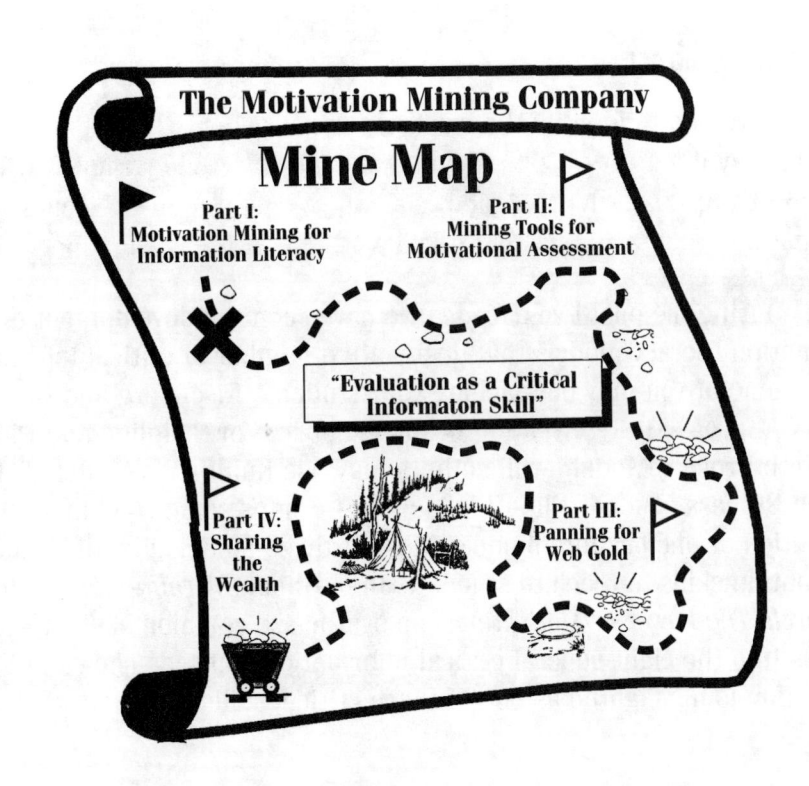

The Motivation Mining Company

Mine Map

Part I: Motivation Mining for Information Literacy

Part II: Mining Tools for Motivational Assessment

"Evaluation as a Critical Informaton Skill"

Part IV: Sharing the Wealth

Part III: Panning for Web Gold

Introduction

The importance of teaching information literacy skills to students is nothing new to the readers of this book. Teachers and library media specialists work individually and collaboratively to integrate information and technology skills into the curriculum and in the context of a current assignment or information need. While this book focuses on motivational evaluation of World Wide Web sites specifically, in Chapter One we begin by looking at evaluation as a critical information literacy skill in general. Then we review the wide variety of resources and services available to educators and students on the Internet and the challenge of evaluating them.

Objectives

When you've completed Chapter One, you will:
- understand the role of evaluation in an information literacy context.
- know about the range of information resources for education on the Internet.
- understand the importance of evaluation of information resources for use in teaching and learning.

Information Literacy

If we had to identify the most important goal of education, we would probably say it is "to develop independent, self-directed learners." With the amount of world knowledge doubling about every three to five years,[1] information literacy becomes a critical attribute of today's independent, self-directed learner.

During the past two decades we have seen the development of several information literacy models that designate a number of critical information skills. Some of you may be teaching your students Eisenberg and Berkowitz's Big Six Approach to Information Problem-Solving[2] or Stripling and Pitts' Research Process Model,[3] while others may use Kuhlthau's Model of the Search Process,[4] Yucht's Flip-It! Model,[5] or perhaps some combination or adaptation of one or more models. Most of these models identify a number of information skills to teach to students. In our book, *Turning Kids on to Research: The Power of Motivation*,[6] we synthesize common skills in existing models into the eight general critical information skills, as shown in Figure 1. Evaluation is highlighted as one of these critical skills.

Fig. 1

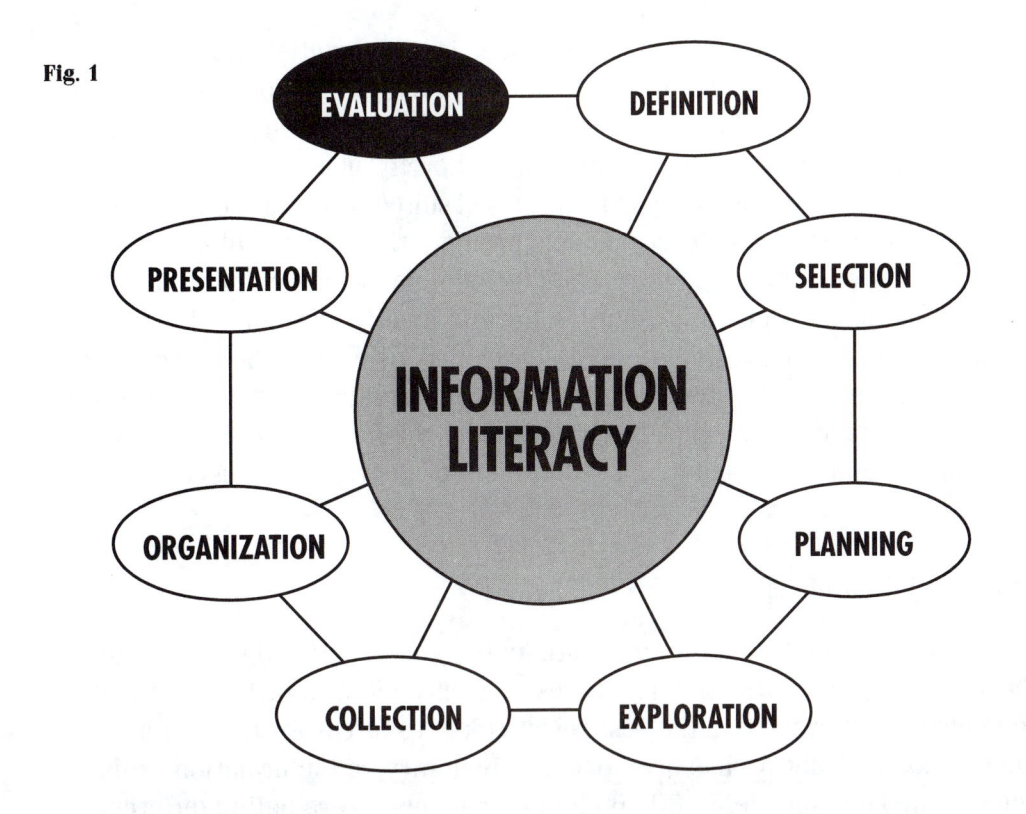

[Diagram: Information Literacy at center, surrounded by eight connected ovals: EVALUATION (highlighted), DEFINITION, SELECTION, PLANNING, EXPLORATION, COLLECTION, ORGANIZATION, PRESENTATION.]

Figure 1: Evaluation is one of the eight critical information literacy skills. (Adapted from Ruth V. Small & Marilyn P. Arnone, *Turning Kids On to Research: The Power of Motivation*, Libraries Unlimited, p. 1-6, 1999.)

Evaluation as an Information Skill

The importance of critical thinking ability, making comparisons, and forming judgments has long been recognized. Benjamin Bloom, in his well-known Taxonomy of Educational Objectives, designated evaluation as the highest form of learning.[7] More recently, the value of developing evaluation skills in even our youngest children has been advocated. For example, the Colorado State Board of Education Goals advocates helping students develop skills for lifelong learning, critical thinking, and the effective use of information; for example, to encourage students "to use multiple sources and types of media to locate, select, evaluate, organize, and present information."[8]

Information Power: Building Partnerships for Learning, the latest version of the national standards for information literacy, designates evaluation as an essential critical thinking skill and describes information literate students as "effective users of ideas and information."[9] *Information Power's* Standard 2 for information literacy states: "The student who is information literate evaluates information critically and competently."[10]

Linda Schamber claims that relevance is the essential criterion in information retrieval and identifies several key factors that contribute to the perceived relevance of documents contained within an information system.[11] Several of these factors (accuracy, credibility, novelty, usefulness, aesthetic value, and difficulty level) are particularly well-suited as evaluation criteria.

Most information literacy models promote the teaching of evaluation skills to children at all grade levels, and include the evaluation of both information and information resources. Several models recommend the evaluation of the *end product* of the research task as well as the *process* used to create that product. The student or an external evaluator, such as the classroom teacher or library media specialist, can conduct this evaluation. Both product and process evaluation require an assessment of the resources used.

Evaluating Information Resources

Information literacy requires students to be able to judge the quality of the wide range of information resources they encounter. In fact, Alice Yucht reminds us that evaluating the *best* resource or resources for a specific information task always has been part of the library and information skills curriculum. For example, The Big6 Model recommends evaluating different sources of information as part of its "information seeking strategies" component. Pappas and Tepe's Pathways to Knowledge Model has an "interpretation" phase in which the student assesses the usefulness and personal relevance of each resource and its information.[12]

Web Sites as Information Resources in Education

Mike Eisenberg states, "Today and in the future, the concept of Library should encompass the full range of information resources—electronic and print."[13] The Internet stands on the verge of becoming *the* main information source, providing students with access to original materials and firsthand information that they never before have had.[14]

The number of schools with Internet access has risen sharply in the past few years. In 1998, a national survey found that 89% of America's schools were connected to the Internet.[15] About 65% of the teachers responding to that survey reported using the Internet in their work, and about 49% of them reported their students using the Internet at least once a week for research.[16] By the year 2000, those statistics likely will rise significantly as the number of Internet-based resources and services available to schools, homes, and libraries continues to rapidly increase.

Web Resources for Teaching and Learning

The Web has become an acceptable, even desirable, information resource in teaching and learning. Web resources used for teaching and learning may contain anything ranging from information on a single topic to databases of text and images on one or more topics, and from lesson plans and single activities to unit plans and curriculum guides with state and national standards mapping. In the 1999 *Educational Media and Technology Yearbook*, Ruth Small and Bernard Lee describe several types of these networked resources.[17]

- **Ask-an-Expert Services.** Dozens of digital Ask-an-Expert services (sometimes called simply "Ask-A" services) that serve the K-12 education community may be found on the Internet.[18] These services handle anything from a broad range of education-related questions (e.g., AskERIC: http://ericir.syr.edu) to a narrowly defined set of content-specific needs (e.g., Ask-a-Volcanologist: http://volcano.und.nodak.edu/vwdocs/ask_a.html). Ask-A services typically provide response information within a reasonable turnaround time.
- **Federal Government Sites.** A number of large databases of educational information are provided by various government agencies and clearinghouses. For example, NASA's site (http://www.nasa.gov) contains information about the universe and space travel for all ages. At the Smithsonian Education Web site, (http://educate.si.edu/lessons/start.html), upper elementary and middle school teachers and students have access to primary sources, museum collections, and materials on subjects ranging from aeronautics to zoology.
- **State Government Sites.** A variety of state-based initiatives have funded the development of educational Web sites that provide a wide range of resources and services to the K-12 community. For example, North Carolina's Department of Public Education Web site features "Tried *n* True Dynamite Lesson Plans" (http://www.ofps.dpi.state.nc.us/OFPS/tc/TNT/index.html) a compilation of model lesson plans linked to state education standards created by teachers for teachers at all levels.
- **Commercial Sites.** A growing number of commercial Web sites are providing free and fee-based services and resources to the K-12 education community. For example, Microsoft's Encarta Online (http://encarta.msn.com/schoolhouse/lessons/default.asp) offers a collection of K-12 lesson plans organized by topics, ranging from fine arts to computers and information technology. Classroom Connect (http://www.classroom.net) offers a searchable database of K-12 educational products, links to lesson plans and other instructional materials, and an Internet searching guide.

▶ **Individual Sites**. An inestimable number of sites have been developed by single individuals and organizations to provide information and activities for teachers and students on a single topic or one or more particular subject areas. The Crayola Crayon Web site (http://www.crayola.com) is a colorful site that offers kids all kinds of art activities. Carol Hurst's Children's Literature Site (http:www.carolhurst.com) provides book reviews, classroom activities, and ideas for using literature within the curriculum. The Weather Dude (http://www.weatherdude.com) provides weather-related information and games.

▶ **Metasites**. There are also a number of Web sites that comprehensively organize other sites on specific subject areas or topics. Mike Tillman calls these "metasites."[19] For example, Math Forum (http://www.forum.swarthmore.edu/) organizes math resources by subject area for all grade levels. Kathy Schrock's Guide for Educators (http://discoveryschool.com/schrockguide/) provides a compilation of Internet sites organized by subject areas, materials to help educators understand basic Internet concepts, links to other Web sites, and tools for helping students and teachers evaluate Web sites. KidsConnect Favorite Sites (http://www.ala.org/ ICONN/kcfavorites.html) provides a list of the favorite Web sites of a group of "cybrarians."

Perhaps the most comprehensive metasite available for educators is the Gateway to Educational Materials (GEM) (http://www.thegateway.org). GEM provides educators with "one-stop, any stop" access to a large range of education-related, Web-based collections, containing thousands of lesson plans, curriculum units, and other Internet-based educational resources.

GEM allows users to search all the collections within its membership by simultaneously using one or more specific criteria (e.g., grade level, subject area, quality level) in order to conduct a more precise search and pinpoint the exact kinds of materials desired. This also saves the time and effort it takes to search each of these collections individually. GEM encompasses both large collections, such as AskERIC's Virtual Library and smaller collections of materials for teaching and learning, such as National Council for Agricultural Education, DramaWest, Tramline Virtual Field Trips, and Computer Curriculum Corporation.

Not only are these electronic resources useful when teaching subject-specific information, but they can also be valuable resources for teaching students a range of information skills. For example, when teaching planning strategies for a student research project (deciding the range of resources that might be used to collect information), one strategy is to use an Ask-A service where students can seek information directly from experts in a particular field.

The explosion of these types of educational materials freely available on the Web has affected both teaching and learning. Laurie Quinlan notes, "Classroom use of the World Wide Web is growing at an astounding pace and affecting the way teachers and students function."[20]

The literature abounds with articles by and about educators who are using electronic resources in their teaching (e.g., for introducing or enriching content) and students who are using Internet resources to conduct research and complete assignments and other learning tasks. For example, Shelley Glantz and Barbara Gorman, a high school English teacher and a library media specialist, collaborated on a lesson that required students to gather information from both print and electronic sources on a current social issue. They would then use the information as evidence in a series of oral debates.[21]

Jerry Schnabel describes an interdisciplinary unit on AIDS that he and his colleagues implemented in which high school health students used the Internet as the primary resource.[22] Dave Berry developed Web-based "guided pages" that he constructed to lead his seventh- and eighth-grade English students to relevant Web sites during lessons about novels.[23] Candace Boyer promotes the use of museum Web sites and other Internet resources as social studies teaching resources;[24] while Frederick and Jean Abel provide examples of ways teachers can use Web sites and other Internet resources to integrate the disciplines of mathematics and social studies.[25]

These are just a few of the hundreds of "stories" you can find in the professional literature. You probably hear many more from your colleagues each day and could likely add some of your own. However, few if any of these stories mention evaluation of the Web sites used, either by the instructor or the students. What are the criteria educators use to select Web sites for their lessons? How do students know they are using high-quality Web sites for their assignments? Unfortunately, the answers to these questions are quite often—"they aren't" and "they don't."

Evaluating Web Resources

Tobias Rademann states "...there has not yet been any kind of quality-control mechanism implemented on the Web, which means that students would definitely have to be taught how to judge the reliability and the value of the various sources they come across..."[26] The importance of "digital literacy," that is, being able to understand and use information from a range of computerized resources, is essential.[27]

Students require a "toolbox" of thinking and problem-solving skills to help them manage what they find. As Jamie McKenzie notes, "the new information landscape requires literacy skills well beyond those needed in previous times, and learners soon find that digital sources are insufficient for many questions and topics."[28]

In our frequent discussions with educators, we hear over and over again about students who conduct an Internet search in the following way:
1. Student enters search keyword.
2. Student retrieves several Web sites.
3. Student takes first Web site listed and leaves.

Does this sound familiar? This would be like a student entering the library, taking the first book off the shelf, and using it to complete an assignment. More often than not, this approach is likely to yield some less than satisfying results.

Unfortunately, the enormous increase of information resources on the Web has not ensured that Web developers will guarantee the validity or quality of their Web sites. This can lead to confusion, frustration, and even chaos. Dave Berry articulately describes such an outcome regarding an attempt to have a group of seventh graders use the Web for research on Shakespeare: "Without the ability to discern the important from the imbecilic among more than 40,000 possible 'Shakespeare' search hits, students foundered in a huge, confusing, and poorly lit 'library.'"[29] Furthermore, teachers sometimes select Web sites to use in their instruction on the basis of "gut feeling" or cursory review of the site; often those sites turn out to be less than adequate for achieving learning objectives and for motivating students.

Therefore, it becomes the responsibility of both students and educators to make informed judgments about the value of a particular site for their needs, based on established evaluative criteria. But the Web is unlike any previous learning medium; it integrates several media simultaneously, provides links to related information that sometimes resides in other sources, and allows the user to select and sequence the information accessed. Thus, the evaluation of networked information resources, such as Web sites, requires a unique set of criteria and new, easy-to-use tools that encompass a broader concept of evaluation.[30]

COMING UP...

In Chapter Two, we discuss the concept of motivation and define what we call *motivation mining* the Web. We also outline the critical factors for a successful Web site and offer a brief glimpse of a newly developed Web evaluation tool that encompasses a broader concept of Web site evaluation.

ENDNOTES

[1] T. Rademann, *Information Unlimited: Employing Internet Resources in Education* <http://www.isoc.org/inet97/proceedings/D3/D3_1.HTM>.

[2] M. B. Eisenberg and R. E. Berkowitz, *Information Problem-solving: The Big Six Skills Approach to Library & Information Skills Instruction*. Norwood, NJ: Ablex Publishing Corp., 1990.

[3] B. K. Stripling and J. M. Pitts, *Brainstorms and Blueprints*. Englewood, CO: Libraries Unlimited, 1988.

[4] C. Kuhlthau, "Implementing a Process Approach to Information Skills: A Study Identifying Indicators of Success in Library Media Programs." *School Library Media Quarterly*, 22 (1), 1993, pp. 11-18.

[5] A. Yucht, *FLIP IT! An Information Skills Strategy for Student Researchers*. Worthington, OH: Linworth Publishing, Inc., 1997.

[6] R. V. Small and M. P. Arnone, *Turning Kids On to Research: The Power of Motivation*. Englewood, CO: Libraries Unlimited, 1999.

[7] B. S. Bloom et al., *Handbook on Formative and Summative Evaluation of Student Learning*. New York: McGraw-Hill, 1971.

[8] P. S. Breivik and J. A. Senn, *Information Literacy: Educating Children for the 21st Century*. New York: Scholastic, 1994, p. 183.

[9] American Association of School Librarians and Association for Educational Communications and Technology. *Information Power: Building Partnerships for Learning*. Chicago: American Library Association, 1998, p. 6.

[10] American Association of School Librarians and Association for Educational Communications and Technology, p. 8.

[11] L. Schamber, "Relevance and information behavior." In M. E. Williams (Ed.). *Annual Review of Information Science and Technology*. Medford, NJ: Learning Information, Inc., 1994.

[12] M. L. Pappas and A. E. Tepe, Follett Information Skills Model. In *Teaching Electronic Information Skills*. McHenry, IL: Follett Software Co., 1995.

[13] M. B. Eisenberg, "Take the Internet Challenge: Using Technology in Context." *Technology Connection-The Book Report-Library Talk*. [Spec. suppl.], September 1996, p. 5.

[14] G. Kearsley, "The World Wide Web: Global Access to Education." *Educational Technology Review*, (5), Winter 1996, pp. 26-30.

[15] "Public Schools with Internet Access Make Significant Strides in 1998," Educational Technology News, 16 (5). Business Publishers, Inc., March 3, 1999, p. 34.

[16] P. Mendels, "Study Shows Students Use Internet Primarily for Research." *The New York Times on the Web*, April 28, 1998. <http://www.nytimes.com/library/tech/98/04/cyber/articles/28education.html>.

[17] R. V. Small and B. Lee, "Web-Based Resources for K-12 Instructional Planning." In R. M. Branch and M. A. Fitzgerald (Eds.), *Educational Media and Technology Yearbook, 24*, 1999, pp. 58-63.

[18] R. D. Lankes and A. S. Kasowitz, *AskA Starter Kit: How to Build and Maintain Digital Reference Services*. Syracuse, NY: ERIC Clearinghouse on Information & Technology, 1998.

[19] M. Tillman, *Education Metasites*. ERIC Clearinghouse on Information & Technology, 1998. (ERIC Document Reproduction Service No. ED 423877)

[20] L. A. Quinlan, "Creating a Classroom Kaleidoscope with the World Wide Web." *Educational Technology, 37* (3), May/June 1997, p. 15.

[21] S. Glantz and B. Gorman, "He Said, She Said: Debating with Technology." *Technology Connection, 4* (7), December 1997, pp. 14-16, 29.

[22] J. Schnabel, "One School's Adventures on the Information Superhighway." *Technology Connection, 2* (9), January 1996, pp. 11, 13.

[23] D. Berry, "Literature on the Web: Guided Searching." *Multimedia Schools*, May/June 1998, pp. 38-41.

[24] C. L. Boyer, "Using Museum Resources in the K-12 Social Studies Curriculum." *ERIC Digest*. Bloomington, IN: ERIC Clearinghouse for Social Studies/Social Science Education, 1996. (ED412174)

[25] F. J. Abel and J. P. Abel, *Integrating Mathematics and Social Studies: Activities Based on Internet Resources*. Paper presented at the Annual Meeting of Teachers of Mathematics, Helena, MT, October 18, 1996.

[26] Rademann, p. 7.

[27] P. Gilster, *Digital Literacy*. New York: Wiley, 1997.

[28] J. McKenzie, "Making WEB Meaning." *Educational Leadership*, 54(3), 1996, pp. 30-32.

[29] Berry, 1998, p. 39.

[30] J. Alexander and M. Tate, "Teaching Web Evaluation." *Internet Trend Watch for Libraries, 3* (2). Librarians and Educators Online, 1998, pp. 49-52,54-55.

HIGHLIGHTS of Chapter One

Here are some of the key points covered in Chapter One.

- ▶ An ultimate goal of education is to develop self-directed learners.
- ▶ The amount of world knowledge doubles about every three to five years.
- ▶ *Information Power* describes information literate students as "effective users of ideas and information" and designates evaluation as an important information skill.
- ▶ Information literacy models promote the evaluation of both information and information resources
- ▶ In 1998, 89% of schools were connected to the Internet.
- ▶ Several types of networked resources and services are available for teaching and learning.
- ▶ The evaluation of networked information resources, such as Web sites, requires new, easy-to-use tools that encompass a broader concept of evaluation.

MINESTORMING

As you were reading, did you think of any new ways you might use Web resources in a future lesson? Use this page to jot down any great thoughts and ideas you have minestormed from Chapter One. "Minestorming" is our word for individual brainstorming (with a "mining twist"). As you continue through this book, you may want to revisit some of these ideas and elaborate on them.

_____
_____
_____
_____
_____
_____
_____
_____
_____
_____

CHAPTER 2

Motivation Mining and the World Wide Web

The Motivation Mining Company

Mine Map

Part I: Motivation Mining for Information Literacy

Part II: Mining Tools for Motivational Assessment

"Motivation Mining and the World Wide Web"

Part IV: Sharing the Wealth

Part III: Panning for Web Gold

Introduction

While the number of World Wide Web sites continues to increase exponentially, so, too, does the need to identify the best sites to use as educational resources. Teachers use Web sites to explain and demonstrate important concepts and principles, and often ask students to use and explore Web sites as part of their assignments. Library media specialists use Web sites to help students locate appropriate resources to complete their assignments. They also incorporate Web sites into their information skills lessons and routinely suggest new sites to teachers and administrators.

Dozens of classroom teachers and library media specialists have told us that at times, no matter how prepared they were to use Web resources in their instruction, how enthusiastic they were about their lesson, and how many effective teaching strategies they used, their lessons still fell short of meeting their objectives. As an educator, you know that even the best-laid plans can go awry, and there may be some other reason for less than excellent outcomes. One reason may be the use of poor-quality Web resources. But, how do we define "quality"?

In this chapter, we will begin to define quality by discussing motivation and its importance for student achievement. We also will introduce the concept of *Motivation Mining*. We'll describe a variety of ways you can motivation mine the Web to identify high-quality Web resources that may be used to enhance both teaching and learning.

Objectives

When you've completed Chapter Two, you will be able to:
- ▶ describe the role of motivation in learning.
- ▶ understand how Web site attributes can affect motivation.
- ▶ explain the concept of *motivation mining*.
- ▶ describe several ways that motivation mining can be useful.
- ▶ describe the relationship between teacher judgments, student perceptions, and Web site attributes in successful Web-based instruction.
- ▶ understand the role of functionality in the context of motivational quality.
- ▶ understand the relationships among teacher judgments, student perceptions, and attributes of Web sites.

Motivation and Learning

Motivation explains the "why" of behavior; that is, why someone chooses one activity over another or spends more time or effort on one task as opposed to another. Sometimes, a person's motivation is based on an external reward such as a grade, an award, or a prize. Other times, it is intrinsic; just participating in an activity or meeting a learning challenge brings satisfaction and pleasure.

Motivation is important in education because research indicates that ability (possessing needed knowledge and skills) does not account for all of the variation in student achievement. In fact, at least some of that variation is due to the learner's motivation. So, motivation is a critical component of learning and especially of the desire for lifelong, self-directed learning. In an information literacy context, Carol Kuhlthau asserts, "One of the key considerations in designing a research task is motivation of students."[1]

One of the most widely known and applied theories of motivation is Expectancy-Value (E-V) Theory.[2] This theory has been described as "one of the most promising models of individual motivation."[3] E-V theory specifies that the amount and quality of effort in a given task or activity depends on two critical prerequisites: (1) *the perceived value of the task* and (2) *an expectation that he or she can be successful in achieving that task*. Therefore, people will not voluntarily put forth effort for a task that holds little or no personal value. Nor will people willingly participate in an activity in which they believe that no matter how hard they try, they are incapable of succeeding. Although originally developed to explain motivation in the work place, recently researchers have found that E-V theory may have appropriate applications in the classroom and in electronic environments.

E-V Theory in the Classroom

Hansen describes four potential student responses to assigned tasks or activities in the context of E-V Theory.[4] If the student values a task *and* has high expectations for success, *engagement* in the activity results (Response 1). However, if the student values the activity but believes there is little or no chance for success, *dissembling* occurs (Response 2). Jere Brophy describes dissembling in this way: "[Students] would like to complete the task successfully, but are uncertain of what to do, how to do it, or whether they can do it. [This causes them to] pretend to understand, make excuses, deny their difficulties, or engage in other behavior..."[5]

On the other hand, if the student has high success expectations but doesn't care about it, the result is *evasion*; that is, doing the minimum required (Response 3). Finally if the student neither values the activity nor has success expectations, the result is often complete *rejection*, a refusal to participate and withdrawal from the activity (Response 4).

You have probably observed or experienced all of these responses in students at one time or another. Some educational theorists have used Expectancy-Value Theory to develop strategies to maximize Response 1 and avoid or minimize Responses 2, 3, and 4. Brophy maintains that much of the research on student motivation may be organized within E-V Theory. He asserts that teachers must (1) help students appreciate the value of learning tasks or activities and (2) make sure that, with a reasonable amount of effort, students can successfully complete these tasks or activities.[6]

One of the most comprehensive applications of E-V theory in education is Keller's ARCS Model of Motivational Design.[7] The ARCS Model specifies four essential factors of motivating instruction: *Attention, Relevance, Confidence,* and *Satisfaction*. Keller maintains that gaining and maintaining *attention* and providing *relevant* resources and activities will increase a student's perceived value of a learning task. Furthermore, providing useful feedback and encouragement, and designing instructional resources or activities that are on the appropriate level of challenge to increase student *confidence*, and rewarding progress toward and achievement of learning goals to foster *satisfaction* will fortify a student's *expectation for success* in a learning task. Keller's model has been one of the most widely applied motivation models for classroom instruction.

E-V Theory in Electronic Environments

Recently, researchers have found that E-V Theory can also be used to explain people's behavior in electronic environments. For example, researchers discovered that E-V Theory was a significant predictor of motivation to use an expert system.[8] They found that the theory was useful early in the design phase to assess the user's intention to use the expert system, which in turn would help guide decisions about the design. E-V Theory has also been found to be valuable for investigating managers' motivation to voluntarily use a computer-based decision support system. Researchers maintain "that users not only need to value potential system-related outcomes, but must also reasonably expect to experience these outcomes as a result of system use."[9]

We believe E-V theory can be effectively applied to a Web environment, as well. Under E-V theory, the user must (1) perceive the Web site as containing relevant and useful information presented in an interesting manner and (2) believe that he or she can successfully navigate the Web site and gain access to needed information. E-V theory also appears to be highly useful as a framework for developing evaluation criteria that identify which features motivate a person to visit, explore, and revisit a Web site.

In fact, *Value* and *Expectation for Success* have a multiplicative function. That is, both factors must be strong for the motivational quality of a Web site to be high. If either factor is absent (or "zero"), then the result is an ineffective Web site because the student will not be motivated to stay and explore or return at another time. Let's think of it in mathematical terms:

VALUE		EXPECTATION FOR SUCCESS		
1	X	0	=	0
0	X	1	=	0
1	X	1	=	SUCCESS!

Motivation Mining: What Is It, and Why Is It Important?

Recently, much attention has been focused on what is termed "data mining" the Web, or what we broadly define as choosing and extracting appropriate, credible, and useful information from the Web. Data mining, in a stricter sense, often involves discovering new or hidden patterns and trends in large databases of information. Sometimes, secret treasures can be found within the vast amounts of information. Uncovering such riches of information can translate into big bucks for the companies that do that research and make use of it.

By the same token, one can discover wonderful treasures to enhance teaching and learning by "motivation mining" the Web. We define motivation mining the Web as the identification and extraction of Web resources that have the potential to enhance student learning by meeting important motivational criteria. These resources provide the content required to complete the task *and* engage and satisfy the Web site user.

Unfortunately, when using the Web, students may have experiences that decrease their motivation. If the research on motivation suggests that students must *also* be motivated in order to learn, then it is not enough that educators *only* judge the appropriateness and authenticity of the content of a specific Web site to guarantee a successful teaching episode. We must *also* be able to determine the motivational aspects for student learning (student judgments of content also affect motivation). Therefore, when measuring the success potential of educational Web resources for teaching, there are three important considerations:

1. *Teachers' judgments* based on expertise in their domain.
2. *Students' perceptions* (and indirectly, educators') of motivational quality.
3. *Web site attributes* that will affect perceptions of motivational quality. In the following sections, we describe the relationship between these factors and the balancing act educators face when assessing Web resources.

Teacher Judgments of Content Validity

Content validity is priority No. 1! Before even considering other motivational concerns, the content must be *appropriate* for your teaching needs. It must support your instructional goals and learning objectives and satisfy the requirements of the activity or assignment. As an educator, you are the best judge of that.

While the content may seem appropriate, it must also be verifiable, that is, valid. So, *authenticity* becomes important. The Web site must contain enough information about the authority source to allow the user to know the credibility of the source and be able to contact that source for clarification or additional information. A number of instruments and a few Web sites that deal very nicely with content issues. One notable one you may wish to explore is Kathy Schrock's Guide for Educators at http://discoveryschool.com/schrockguide. This and other evaluation instruments are briefly discussed in Chapter 3.

We also have developed a brief instrument for educators to measure content validity. The Content Validity Checklist (see Appendix C) is intended to be used to screen Web sites for inclusion in lesson plans.

When lesson-planning, it is the responsibility of the educator to decide whether a specific Web site measures up to its content validity criteria. An educator's judgment of appropriate and authentic content is a **necessary** but **insufficient** condition for a successful teaching episode. We think you know where this is going.

Students' Perceptions of Motivational Quality

Many teachers and library media specialists have told us about the times they were well-prepared, presented their lessons in an enthusiastic manner, and used what are considered to be excellent teaching strategies, but still felt their lessons were not successful in terms of achieving their objectives. Consider the following example:

> *I thought I had found the "perfect" Web site to spice up my lesson on cell division, but my students seemed to have a different reaction. Although the Web site's information was on an appropriate level and potentially useful, the site failed to maintain the students' attention and interest, which defeated my purpose for using it. Many complained that the way the information was presented was dull and the Web site was boring. Most of them just tuned out!*
>
> — A 10th grade biology teacher

Students' perceptions of the motivational quality of a Web site, and indirectly, the teacher or library media specialist's best estimate of students' potential perceptions of motivational quality, are critical factors in a successful teaching episode using Web resources. That is, will the experience of interacting with the particular Web site you have chosen help motivate your students to learn? Will they want to stay in the Web site, look for links to related resources, and possibly revisit the Web site for future learning opportunities after your lesson is over? Motivational quality can make or break a lesson. *Students' perceptions of* motivational quality will ultimately determine the effectiveness of a Web site as a teaching/learning resource.

A Web site resource with high motivational quality enhances the learning process. The degree of motivational quality is especially important if the student is doing independent research and has a choice between two or more Web sites to visit and use. It is also important for the educator who is selecting Web sites for use in teaching or student assignments.

A Web Site's Motivational Attributes: The Pivotal Factor

A Web site's motivational attributes will influence both student and teacher perceptions of motivational quality. In the context of E-V theory, how stimulating and meaningful a Web site is contribute to its perceived value; features that demonstrate that the Web site is organized and easy-to-use promote a positive expectation for success. The degree to which these qualities are present comprises the *motivational quality* of that Web site. Later in this chapter, we will explore these attributes further in the section entitled "Web Sites That Have What It Takes."

When judging a Web site's attributes and their effect on motivational quality, we certainly are not only talking about features that provide glitz or "fluff." The *Value* (E-V Theory) issues include content criteria for judging the information contained within a Web site. These include accuracy, currency, clarity, validity, and comprehensive coverage of the topic. You are probably wondering, "Aren't these the content validity criteria that were discussed under 'teacher judgments'?" Although they are content-related criteria, they can also have an effect on student motivation and therefore must also be included in a Web evaluation instrument that focuses on motivational quality. A Web site that contains accurate and unbiased information provided by credible sources, increases the value of that site for the student. Conversely, a student may become frustrated at not finding enough or the right kind of information for his needs. In Part II, you will see that content issues are naturally addressed in the instrument and framed in terms of their effect on motivation.

But, what about functionality—those features, such as navigation buttons and hot links that make the Web site work the way it should? When functional features don't work, the results might be similar to the following gripe.

When teaching our ninth graders about location and access strategies with electronic resources, I often run into situations where a student does a search and comes up with dozens of sites on a topic. At first, the student is excited but soon becomes anxious when some of the sites just don't work right, many of the links are broken and the number of graphics result in an unreasonable amount of loading time. Often that student becomes frustrated and quits, or just arbitrarily chooses a couple of Web sites to use.

— A high school library media specialist

The situation above illustrates how successful searching on the Web can often turn into information overload and can create a level of frustration in students that often discourages the very curiosity and information exploration you had hoped to stimulate. Functionality is an important issue, especially since it affects motivation. When functionality is discussed in this book, then, it is framed in terms of its *effect on motivation.*

Some of the participants in our summer seminar identified some successful Web sites that exemplified both value *and* expectation for success by providing high content validity and motivational quality. Kendra Sikop evaluated her local county's online newspaper site. Here is part of her evaluation:

[This Web site's] overall organization offers several search options that provide users with plenty of options, [such as] lots of pull-down menus and hypertext to point and click and go! The Web site is enjoyable to explore and will sustain interest... [It] clearly states its purpose, objectives, and intended audience on the home page. Several unique features that add value to the Web site include searching for back issues of the newspaper and the ability to search by town for tag sales.

Besides the newspaper stories, there are many additional features to aid the informational needs of the community, such as [the] dining guide, and the ability to search by business type, (for example, automotive and wedding services). The Web site also provides a forum for feedback that satisfies the need for interactivity and opportunities for individual and cooperative group use. The user also has the ability to send email to the newspaper's main departments, including to the [newspaper's] director and editor. Links to other relevant sites are available and include access to local library home pages as well as other Internet links...

[The site] informs users how often information is updated. By using this site, I could learn of job postings before the paper hits the streets! A user can search for specific words in the classified ads and, if the user does not find what he or she is looking for,

can request to be notified automatically if any future ads meet the user's search criteria. Another value-added feature available on this Web site is the ability to mark interesting classified ads. [This site was] informative and fun to use!

This Web site certainly met the criteria for both content validity and motivational quality. As an online version of a reputable newspaper, it satisfied the validity criterion. As Kendra pointed out, it added value to its paper counterpart with such features as keyword searching capability and speedy updating of information, and thus increased credibility.

The site also receives high marks for motivational quality. Its use of pull-down menus and hypertext makes this site more engaging; while the inclusion of information that meets the needs of its users and providing the ability to search by keyword, mark important information, and link to relevant sites adds to the meaningfulness of this site. The site's overall organization and the use of the feedback forum, the e-mail capability, and other features increase the user's satisfaction and expectations for successful use of this site. Kendra's evaluation may give you some ideas about what attributes contribute to Web sites that "have what it takes."

For successful teaching episodes, the educator must judge the content of the selected Web site to be appropriate and authentic. We assume that you, as the educator, are familiar with the specific content you have selected for a lesson and will make certain that whatever Web site you are considering using in your classroom or library media center has appropriate and authentic content. The motivational quality should be high. Motivational quality is based on students' perceptions of value and expectation for success. These perceptions are influenced by the Web site's attributes. Educators should also be able to project a Web site's potential motivational impact on students. We summarize the previous sections of this chapter by presenting a visual model that depicts the relationship between *teacher* judgments of content validity, *student* perceptions based on motivational quality, and *attributes* in a Web site design that influence motivational quality. We call it the TSA Model for Web-Based Instruction (see Figure 2).

Fig. 2

[Diagram: TSA Model for Web-Based Instruction©

Dependent on Both: CONTENT VALIDITY / MOTIVATIONAL QUALITY

CONTENT VALIDITY — Based on Teacher Judgements of: Appropriateness, Authenticity

MOTIVATIONAL QUALITY — Based on Student Perceptions of: Value, Expectation for Success

Influenced by Web Site Attributes: Stimulating, Meaningful, Organized, Easy to Use]

©Marilyn P. Arnone & Ruth V. Small,
The Motivation Mining Company, 1999.

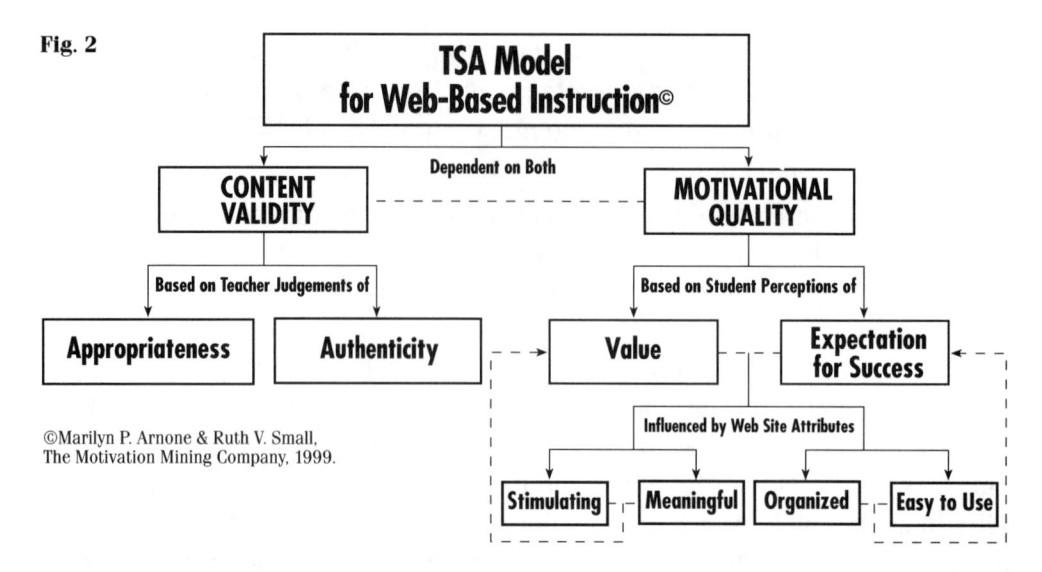

Figure 2: The TSA Model illustrates the relationship between teacher judgments, student perceptions, and attributes of Web sites in using Web resources. ©Marilyn P. Arnone & Ruth V. Small, The Motivation Mining Company, 1999.

Web Sites That Have What It Takes

Earlier in the chapter, we discussed some of the attributes of Web sites that make them "valuable assets" (in motivation mining terms) to your lesson plans. No let's go into a bit more detail about those attributes. Figure 3 illustrates the relationship between four motivational quality attributes and E-V theory.

Fig. 3

[Diagram: Stimulating, Meaningful → Value; Organized, Easy to Use → Expectation for Success]

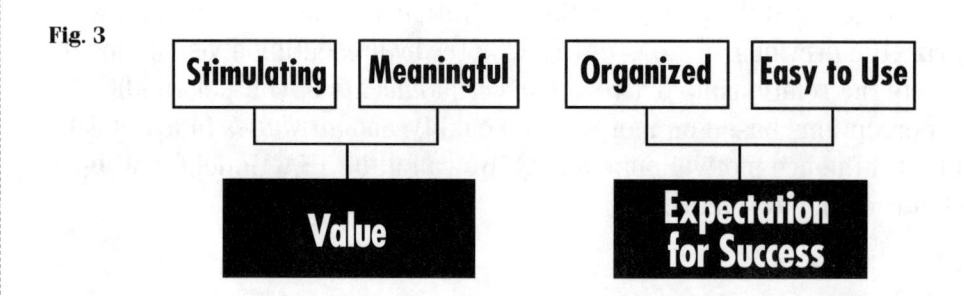

Figure 3: Four motivational quality attributes related to Value and Expectation for Success.

A *Stimulating* Web site includes features that both capture and maintain interest and curiosity. These features are especially important for engaging learners. *Meaningful* refers to the usefulness, credibility, and personal relevance of the Web site to the student. For example, the authenticity of the site's content and its appropriateness for the designated audience would relate to personal relevance. These features all relate to the *Value* component of E-V theory.

Attributes such as menus, site maps, navigation aids, user control, and help mechanisms translate into an *organized* and *easy-to-use* Web site. Such features help to build confidence in the student's ability to have a successful experience with the Web site. These features relate to the *Expectation for Success* component of E-V theory.

Putting It All Together

We summarize this chapter by presenting a visual model that depicts the relationships between *teacher* judgments of content suitability, *student* perceptions based on motivational quality, and *attributes* in a Web site design that influence motivational quality. We call it the TSA Model for Web-Based Instruction. Using E-V theory as its core, the TSA Model provides the theoretical foundation for our Web evaluation instruments described in upcoming chapters.

COMING UP...

In Part II, Chapter Three, we'll discuss the *WebMAC Senior* motivational assessment tool and describe its development and testing.

ENDNOTES

[1] C. Kuhlthau, *Teaching the Library Research Process*. West Nyack, NY: The Center for Applied Research in Education Inc., 1985, p. 7.

[2] V. H. Vroom, *Work and Motivation*. San Francisco: Jossey-Bass, 1995.

[3] F. G. Burton, Y. Chen, V. Grover, and K. A. Stewart, "An Application of Expectancy Theory for Assessing User Motivation to Utilize an Expert System. *Journal of Management Information Systems, 9* (3), Winter 1992-3, pp. 183-198.

[4] D. Hansen, "Lesson Evading and Lesson Dissembling: Ego Strategies in the Classroom." *American Journal of Education, 97,* 1989, pp. 184-208.

[5] J. Brophy, *Motivating Students to Learn*. Boston: McGraw-Hill, 1998, p. 16.

[6] J. Brophy, 1998.

[7] J. M. Keller, "Strategies for Stimulating the Motivation to Learn." *Performance & Instruction, 26* (8), October 1987, pp. 1-7.

[8] Burton et al., 1992-3.

[9] K. C. Snead, Jr., and A. M. Harrell. "An Application of Expectancy Theory to Explain a Manager's Intention to Use a Decision Support System." *Decision Sciences, 25* (4), 1995, p. 508.

HIGHLIGHTS of Chapter Two

Here are some key points covered in Chapter Two.

▶ Motivation explains why someone chooses one activity over another or spends more time or effort on one task than another.

▶ Motivation is an important factor in student achievement.

▶ Motivation mining is the identification and extraction of Web resources that have the potential to enhance student learning by meeting important motivational criteria.

▶ There are two major factors to consider when assessing Web sites: content validity and motivational quality. High-quality Web sites require the presence of both factors.

▶ High motivational quality requires strong value and expectation for success attributes. Value attributes make a Web site stimulating and meaningful. Expectation for success attributes mean a Web site is organized and easy-to-use.

▶ The theoretical foundation for our Web evaluation instruments has E-V theory at its core and focuses on the relationship between teacher judgments of content validity, student perceptions of value and expectation for success, and Web site attributes.

MINESTORMING

You've probably had the experience of planning a lesson, selecting what you thought was the perfect Web site for an activity, and then finding the it just didn't work the way you had hoped. Is it possible that the Web site lacked motivational quality? What might you do differently next time? What could you suggest to improve the Web site's appeal, if anything? Use this page to jot down great thoughts and ideas you have minestormed from Chapter Two. Then read on.

_____

_____

_____

_____

_____

_____

_____

_____

_____

_____

PART II

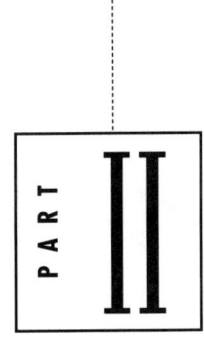

Mining Tools for a Motivational Assessment

CHAPTER 3

Using a Motivational Assessment Tool to Evaluate Web Resources

The Motivation Mining Company
Mine Map

Part I: Motivation Mining for Information Literacy

Part II: Mining Tools for Motivational Assessment

"Using a Motivational Assessment Tool to Evaluate Web Resources"

Part IV: Sharing the Wealth

Part III: Panning for Web Gold

Introduction

Only a few of the numerous Web evaluation tools available are designed for use by children and also focus on the motivational aspects of Web sites, such as those features that motivate students to visit, stay and explore, and return to a Web site. In Chapter Three, we describe some existing Web site evaluation instruments, present the theoretical foundation for the *Website Motivational Analysis Checklist*© assessment tool and describe the development and testing of the instrument.

Objectives

By the end of this chapter, you will:
▶ be familiar with several Web site evaluation instruments.
▶ understand the differences between the *WebMAC* instruments and other Web evaluation instruments.

Existing Web Evaluation Instruments

Because of their dynamic, interactive nature, Web sites require different criteria for evaluation than some of the other more traditional types of media (e.g., print, video). Several excellent evaluation instruments are available to help educators judge the suitability of a Web site for instructional needs. Some focus heavily on content and validity issues (Does it have the right information?), while others focus on functionality issues (Does it work the way it is supposed to?).

Most of these instruments, with the exception of Kathy Schrock's, were designed for use by librarians and teachers to assess the appropriateness of Web sites. Only a handful were created for students to use independently or for educators to use as a tool for teaching students a structured method for evaluating Web sites. Furthermore, few are theoretically based and offer diagnostic methods for assessing and interpreting results. In the following paragraphs, we'll briefly introduce some other Web evaluation instruments, and point out how they differ from the instruments presented in this book. We encourage readers to visit any or all of these Web sites and review them in more depth.

Carolyn Caywood's *Library Selection Criteria for WWW Resources* instrument specifies evaluation criteria in three categories (access, design, and content). Each category contains a comprehensive list of related questions. The tool is designed to aid librarians in assessing a Web site's value to its users

There is no scoring mechanism included, and the analysis and interpretation process is not described. (http://www6.pilot.infi.net/~carolyn/criteria.html)

Esther Grassian's *Thinking Critically About World Wide Web Resources* instrument has four categories of "points to consider" (Content & Evaluation; Source & Date; Structure; and Other). The author provides helpful links to additional resources, including "Guiding Children Through Cyberspace—URL's," a page that lists Web sites for guiding children's home use of the Internet (e.g., software reviews, ratings of Web sites). There is no scoring mechanism, and no analysis/interpretation method is included. (http://www.library.ucla.edu/libraries/college/instruct/)

Karen McLachlan developed a set of three Web evaluation instruments called *Cyberguides*. Two instruments rate content, and a third evaluates Web site design. Each instrument consists of eight general areas of assessment (e.g., speed, content/information) with several criteria for each area (e.g., "The home page downloads efficiently enough to use during whole class instruction," "The information is clearly labeled and organized, and will be easily understood by my students"). Her instruments use a numerical rating system and include an interpretation of one's total score, but do not break that score down by category or item or provide visual representation of scores. (http://www.cyberbee.com/guides.html)

Kathy Schrock has developed three versions of her *Critical Evaluation Survey* for students at different levels (elementary, middle, secondary). Each instrument begins by asking the student some questions about how they accessed the site and what site they are evaluating. The elementary school version contains 18 main questions, the middle school version has 24 main questions, and the secondary school version has 35 main questions. Most questions are answered with a simple "yes" or "no." All versions ask for qualitative summary responses. No scoring mechanism or analysis/interpretation method is included. (http://discoveryschool.com/schrockguide/evalmidd.html)

All of these instruments are useful for evaluating Web sites. Recently, however, we developed a unique set of evaluation instruments that focus on *motivational quality* while encompassing content and functionality issues from a motivational perspective. Each of these instruments has a detailed scoring and interpretation process with graphs and grids for representing scores visually. Furthermore, these instruments were created primarily for children to use independently or for adults to use as instructional tools to help students learn to evaluate Web sites.

The Website Motivational Analysis Checklist

The *Website Motivational Analysis Checklist*© (known as *WebMAC*, for short) series of Web evaluation instruments, designed for evaluators from grade 1 to adult, is based on expectancy-value theory applied to the Web environment. The series includes instruments specifically created for use in educational, business, or entertainment contexts. These instruments have been thoroughly tested and validated, which has resulted in several major revisions and modifications to the original instrument. The *WebMAC* instruments are intended to identify areas for improvement of an existing Web site and provide guidance for the design of a new Web site. They are widely used as materials in teaching students to evaluate Web resources.

A set of eight instruments was developed. These instruments distinguish themselves from existing Web evaluation instruments because they:

▶ are student-centered.
▶ are theoretically based.
▶ focus on motivational issues.
▶ have been tested and validated.
▶ incorporate a variety of methods for analysis and interpretive feedback.

Each of the instruments contains items on important aspects of evaluation, such as content credibility, currency, navigation, links, and organization. In some way, each of these aspects has a major impact on motivation which accounts for student behaviors such as persistence on task (e.g., amount of time a student will continue to explore for information at a given site), and whether a student will return to a site to learn more at another time.

Let's take the content credibility aspect of evaluating Web sites. A Likert-type agreement scale such as *WebMAC Senior*, for example, includes this item related to content credibility: "The information contained in this Web site is current and up-to-date." In motivational terms, this item relates to the *Value* dimension. Discovering you had outdated information for a school project would be frustrating and discouraging; a student's motivation would decrease and a return visit to that site would be unlikely.

Items like "All buttons and other navigation mechanisms for moving around at this Web site worked the way they should" refer to the navigational aspects of Web sites. In terms of motivation, how easy or difficult it is to navigate impacts a student's confidence and expectation that he or she can be successful in a particular Web site environment. When these mechanisms do not work the way they should, they cause frustration and boredom.

So, in using the *WebMAC* instruments, you will see many items that relate to the critical evaluation issues that we are all concerned about; the *WebMAC* instruments, however, take such concerns to another level by framing them in motivational terms. This serves a twofold purpose in education: It makes the instruments valuable to both (1) students who are learning evaluation skills, and (2) educators who use the instruments as lesson-planning and design tools and must consider the all-important contribution of motivation to learning.

WebMAC Senior

The *Website Motivational Analysis Checklist (WebMAC) Senior*© was designed for use by students in grade nine and up. *WebMAC Senior* may be used by an individual student or an entire class. The instrument allows the student to rate the motivational quality of various aspects of a Web site and plot the scores on a grid, allowing quick visual assessment of the strengths and weaknesses of that site. The reasonable length of the instrument permits students to easily pinpoint specific areas in need of improvement.

WebMAC Senior has many uses beyond teaching evaluation skills. The instrument may also be used by teachers for selecting Web sites to use in their lessons or as guidelines for developing new Web sites or improving existing ones. In this book, we focus on the use of *WebMAC Senior* with high school students and, in Chapter Eight we offer some ideas for using this instrument in the context of information literacy instruction, integrated with the curriculum. The instrument and directions for administering, scoring, and interpreting results are featured in the next four chapters of this book.

Other WebMAC Instruments

WebMAC Senior is one of eight *WebMAC* instruments. The other *WebMAC* instruments are:
▶ *WebMAC Junior*©*: a Web evaluation tool for students in grades one through four. It was designed to help our youngest students diagnose, analyze, and assess Web sites *from a child's perspective*. *WebMAC Junior's* administration guidelines include definitions of several common Web site

---

*A 24-item version of this instrument (*WebMAC Junior: Long Form*©) is also available. An abbreviated form containing 12 items, *Website Investigator*© (Arnone & Small, 1999), is intended for very young children.

terms (e.g., home page, button, link), a brief overview of its theoretical foundation, ideas for curriculum-related activities, and step-by-step directions for completing and scoring the instrument.

WebMAC Junior contains a total of 16 items (eight *Value*; eight *Expectation for Success*) in question form and uses smiley faces for recording responses. Scores may be visually represented on scoring grids. Examples of *WebMAC Junior* items for each category are:

VALUE: *Was what you found on this Web site useful to you?*

EXPECTATION FOR SUCCESS: *Was it easy to find your way around the different parts of this Web site?*

WebMAC Junior is featured in our companion book, *WWW Motivation Mining: Finding Treasures for Teaching Evaluation Skills (Grades 1-6).*[1] This book also includes *WebMAC Junior: Long Form* and a variety of ideas elementary teachers and library media specialists submitted for using *WebMAC Junior* with students.

▶ *WebMAC Middle©*: similar in format to *WebMAC Senior* but targets students in grades 5-8. (This instrument is included in its entirety in Appendix B of this book.) It contains 24 statements (12 Value; 12 Expectation for Success). Like its high school counterpart, items are scored using a four-point scale from "0" (strongly disagree) to "3" (strongly agree). However, *WebMAC Middle* has no Not Applicable (NA) designation and uses only two dimensions (Value and Expectation for Success). Examples of *WebMAC Middle* statements for each category are:

VALUE: *"I like the colors and backgrounds used at this Web site."*

EXPECTATION FOR SUCCESS: *"I find this Web site to be well-organized."*

Students then tally their scores for the two dimensions and plot them on the scoring grid for quick and easy visual interpretation. The complete *WebMAC Middle* instrument with scoring directions, grids, and tally sheets is included in Appendix B. The tool is intended for use by middle and junior high school educators or by high school educators who wish to use a simpler instrument with their students.

▶ *WebMAC Professional©*: designed for professional educators, Web designers, instructional designers, and others to use when participating in a Web site review panel. Its purpose is to assess the motivational effectiveness of Web sites targeted toward educators.

▶ *WebMAC Broadcast/Cable©*: created for children's television producers to use to assess their program-related Web sites. The instrument has 28 items and contains many of the same questions as *WebMAC Junior: Long Form*, plus additional ones pertaining specifically to television programs.

▶ *WebMAC Business©*: an instrument businesses can use to assess their commercial Web sites. This instrument is currently in its final stages of testing and revision.

Development and Testing

The *WebMAC* instruments have been continuously tested since they were first developed in 1997. Close to 100 preservice and inservice classroom teachers and library professionals (and more than 600 students) have participated in their pilot testing. Pilot testing allowed us to identify vague or inconsistent language, redundant items, length of time to complete, and level of ease of directions for administering and scoring. Following each test, *WebMAC Senior* was revised and refined and eventually modified from 60 to 40 items. The instrument has also undergone extensive statistical analysis, using factorial analyses to verify clustering of items into proposed categories. As a result, *WebMAC Senior* was modified for a final time from a 40-item version to its current 32-item design.

With the widespread adoption and use of the *WebMAC* instruments by teachers and library media specialists around the country and internationally, we continue to receive positive feedback and ideas for improvement. Even in the earliest stages of evaluating the *WebMAC* instruments, comments from pilot testers were overwhelmingly positive. Some of their comments appear below:

"...very informative and a good tool."

"...questions were very easy to answer."

"...simple to use, self scoring, and easy to interpret."

"...an excellent tool to use to really evaluate a site for its true value."

"...not very time-consuming in the execution phase, and allowed for the person using them to 'surf' the site and then fill them in, instead of being intrusive and interfering with the site visit."

"...this instrument was very well designed and functional... easy to understand and use."

"...very thorough, yet not too long."

"...filling it out was a satisfying experience in itself; I enjoyed reflecting about my experience of the site."

"I also see [the instrument] as an excellent tool to use to help students learn for themselves how to judge the quality of different Web sites."

Three Ways To Use Web Site Motivational Assessment

There are a number of ways you can use the Web site motivational assessment tools provided in this book. As we present each of these ways, we will provide a scenario that illustrates its application.

1. A TEACHING TOOL

You can use *WebMAC Senior* as a teaching tool to help your students learn valuable evaluation skills. In this way, they will understand how important evaluation can be when it comes to electronic resources on the Web, and you can guarantee that they are using high-quality resources.

> **SCENARIO**
>
> Dan Belen, a middle school library media specialist, collaborated with the seventh grade math team to plan a lesson that integrates math and information skills, specifically evaluation. The students were required to work in pairs and use both print and Web resources to research a famous mathematician. They were also asked to develop a multimedia presentation to present at the school's upcoming Math Fair.
>
> Dan has been working with these students on their information skills since fifth grade. This year he is emphasizing evaluation skills, one of their weaker areas. Although students understand that the resources they use in the library have undergone a rigorous selection process, they need to know that the resources they find on the Internet have had no such scrutiny. So Dan and the teachers agree that the students should use *WebMAC Senior* for each Web resource they ultimately use in their presentations.
>
> Before the students begin their research, Dan leads a discussion on the importance of Web evaluation and teaches the students how to use *WebMAC Senior*. He shows them an example of a Web site that he has evaluated using the instrument and then has them practice individually with a couple of sites. Each class plots their scores on the scoring grid, providing a perfect (and more meaningful) exercise to practice the graphing skills they were learning in class.
>
> As the students use *WebMAC Senior* to evaluate the Web sites they encounter in their research, some are surprised to find that what appears to be a site designed by a subject matter expert is actually a site developed by some high school students. Others find sites that are poorly organized, difficult to navigate and with many inactive links. By using a comprehensive instrument to assess Web site motivational quality, the students can identify which sites to incorporate into their presentations and gather evidence to justify their decisions. Dan, the math teachers, and the students are pleased with the results.

2. A Lesson-Planning Tool

Using the Web in classroom presentations or as part of student activities and assignments has become commonplace. But how do you know if the Web sites you have chosen are high-quality sites? You don't, unless you evaluate them. So, you may also find *WebMAC Senior* useful as a *lesson-planning tool* to help you make important decisions about whether a particular site may or may not be appropriate for your teaching objectives, not only from a content validity perspective but also from a motivational perspective. Here's another scenario to illustrate the use of *WebMAC Senior* in this way.

SCENARIO

In response to publicity and the interest of her students, tenth grade biology teacher Rachel Cohen a is planning a lesson on cloning. The lesson will kick off a project in which students will have to conduct research in order to debate the issues related to the topic. She wants to begin with a dynamic lesson, and she is looking for materials to help her plan and implement her instruction.

When Rachel types the keyword into a search engine, she receives dozens of potential Web sites with text, audio, and video information, which she wants to incorporate into her lesson. Rachel knows she can't use them all, so she uses *WebMAC Senior* to help her identify the most credible and motivating sites on her topic and decide which ones to integrate into the lesson. Rachel is able to narrow her search down to four "Awesome Web Sites."

---

3. A Research and Design Tool

You may also find *WebMAC Senior* valuable as a *research and design tool*. You can use it to conduct your own research comparing the motivational effectiveness of various sites that contain the same type of content. Or, you may be interested in researching the effect of motivational quality of Web sites on learning outcomes. You or your students may use the tool's items as guidelines for designing your own class or school Web site.

Here is our final scenario that illustrates the use of *WebMAC Senior* for research and design. We will highlight additional examples of the application of *WebMAC Senior* to each of these three contexts in Chapters Eight and Nine. These examples were provided by practitioners and researchers who have been using *WebMAC Senior* in various ways.

SCENARIO

Greg Cooper is the high school technology teacher and adviser to the school's Technology Club. He is working with the Club to design the school's Web site. Greg asks each of the students to identify one or two exemplary existing school Web sites by using *WebMAC Senior* to rate the sites they find. Greg then meets with the students to discuss the design of their Web site, incorporating some of their favorite features from the exemplary sites with their own original ideas. After the students complete the initial development of their school's Web site, Greg arranges with the English teachers to have their classes evaluate the Web site and share the results with the Club. The English teachers have their students use *WebMAC Senior* to assess the fledgling site. Each class tallies and plots its scores on the *WebMAC* grid. The Technology Club uses the general results and the item analysis to improve and enhance specific features at their site before finally posting it to the Web and announcing the site to the rest of the school.

COMING UP...

In the next three chapters, you'll find everything you'll need to use *WebMAC Senior* with your students. We begin with complete administration directions in Chapter Four.

ENDNOTES

[1] M. P. Arnone and R. V. Small, *WWW Motivation Mining: Finding Treasures for Teaching Evaluation Skills (Grades 1-6)*. Linworth Publishing, Inc., 1999.

HIGHLIGHTS of Chapter Three

Here are some of the key points covered in Chapter Three.

▶ A number of highly effective Web evaluation instruments are available for use in education.
▶ The *Website Motivational Analysis Checklist (WebMAC)* instruments are student-centered and theoretically-based, and they focus on motivational issues.
▶ The *WebMAC* instruments have been tested and validated with educators and students.
▶ The *WebMAC* instruments incorporate mechanisms for analysis and interpretation.
▶ Several *WebMAC* instruments were developed for educational use: *WebMAC Senior* for students in grades 9 and up, *WebMAC Middle* for grades 5-8, and *WebMAC Junior, Website Investigator,* and *WebMAC Junior: Long Form* for students in grades 1-4.
▶ The three main ways to use *WebMAC Senior* are as a teaching tool, as a lesson-planning tool, and as a research and design tool.

MINESTORMING

In this chapter, you learned that *WebMAC Senior* has several uses. Did any of these stimulate ideas about how you plan to use the instrument? Feel free to use this page to jot down any great thoughts and ideas you have minestormed from Chapter Three.

_____
_____
_____
_____
_____
_____
_____
_____
_____
_____

CHAPTER 4

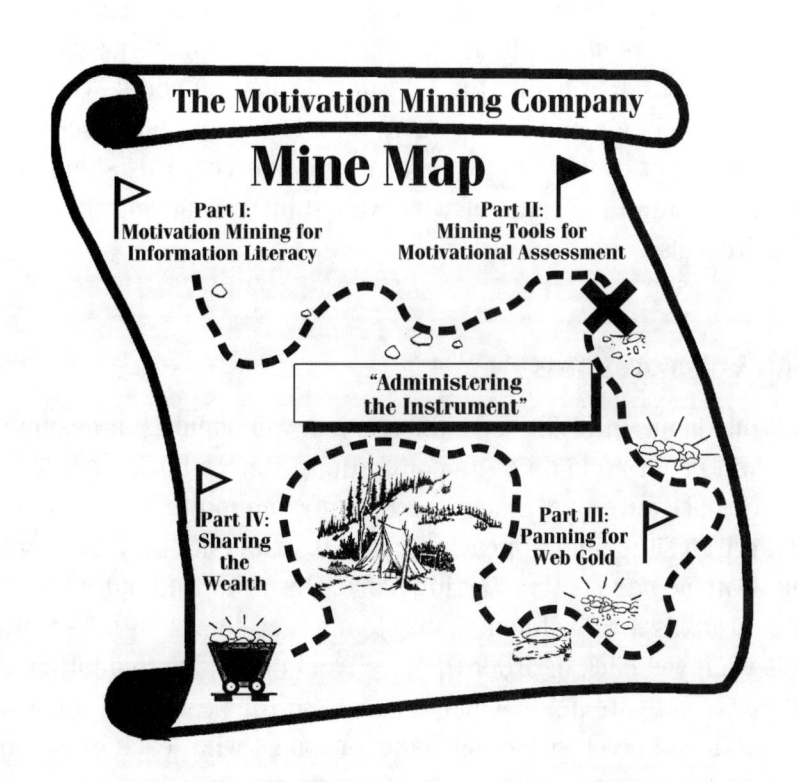

Administering the Instrument

The Motivation Mining Company
Mine Map

Part I: Motivation Mining for Information Literacy

Part II: Mining Tools for Motivational Assessment

"Administering the Instrument"

Part IV: Sharing the Wealth

Part III: Panning for Web Gold

Introduction

The *Website Motivational Analysis Checklist (WebMAC)* for high school students *(WebMAC Senior)* is intended to assess the motivational quality of a Web site—its appeal, usefulness, and ease of use. In this chapter, you will find complete directions for administering *WebMAC Senior* to your students or for using it yourself.

Objectives

By the end of this chapter, you will understand:
▶ how to complete the *WebMAC Senior* instrument.
▶ how to administer the *WebMAC Senior* instrument to students.
▶ how *WebMAC Senior* can be taught in the larger context of evaluation of information resources.

Why Evaluation?

While preparing this book, we found that many students (and even some teachers) have never even considered the importance of evaluation of Web resources. Some wonder why evaluation of Web resources is necessary. Several practitioners have told us (as you will see in Chapter Eight) that many students believe that "if it's on the Internet, it must be good!" Therefore, it may be useful to begin any lesson on Web evaluation with a discussion about why it is important to learn to evaluate Web resources. This should help students understand the value of Web evaluation in ensuring the quality of the resources they use.

Defining Common Terms

While home Internet use is increasing, you should not assume that students will understand all of its conventions. Before having students review a Web site, make sure they understand some common terms used in discussing Web sites (and appearing in the instruments they will use). For example, a *home page* is the starting place. Here you find out what is on the Web site. A *link* is a way of connecting to another source of information. A *button* is what you click in order to move from one place to another within the Web site or to activate a particular request. Buttons can be of any shape or size, but it should be clear by their label or image what each one is meant to do. You could give them the example of a picture of a house icon commonly used as a button to bring the student back to the *home page*.

Defining common terms may not be necessary with older students or students who already have experience with the World Wide Web. Those who are not "Web savvy" may feel too embarrassed to admit their inexperience. Sometimes, it is helpful to simply call it a "review."

Providing an Overview

Once students are comfortable with Web site conventions and terminology, you can provide them with an overview of the specific site that students will evaluate. You may use the following suggestions:
▶ Discuss the general topic or subject matter of the Web site. For example, if the Web site is science-related, briefly tell the students what to expect.
▶ Give students a few minutes to explore the Web site so they can gain some preliminary familiarity with its basic content and structure before they really take the time to explore. You can either give them a couple of minutes to do this on their own or with a small group, or you can demonstrate it yourself if everyone is evaluating the same Web site.

Interacting with the Web Site

We found educators like to use two basic approaches when teaching students how to use *WebMAC Senior* within a single period. Some prefer to give students about 15-20 minutes to explore and interact with the Web site. Students either do this individually or within a small group. After giving students this free exploration time, they provide each student or small group with *WebMAC Senior*. They then allow time for students to read the directions for the instrument and to complete the items. This is the approach Marilyn Natke took when she taught students to use *WebMAC Middle*, as you will see in Chapter Eight.

The second approach is to hand out *WebMAC Senior* first and ask students to read the directions for the instrument on their own. Then allow them to explore and interact with the Web site and fill out the instrument as they wish. When using this approach, students will need more time as they are exploring and using the checklist at the same time. This approach works best for older students or those who already have experience using the instrument and who can complete the instrument independently.

These are the two basic approaches most commonly used by educators. It may take place as a standalone lesson or, as we recommend, integrated into a curriculum-related unit. You may think of yet another approach that will work best with your students.

Giving Students Directions

If you wish to take a peek at *WebMAC Senior* in Chapter Five, feel free to do so because it may help you become familiar with some of the items before reading on. It might be useful to read the directions aloud, including the example item, so that students understand clearly that *WebMAC Senior* is *not* a test but rather a way for them to hone their skills as critical evaluators. Be sure to emphasize that there are *no wrong answers*, and many questions require their opinions and independent judgments. It seems even older students can have a difficult time with this because they are so accustomed to standardized tests with only one right answer to a question. You also may want to take a minute or two to make sure the "Not Applicable" designation is fully understood.

Some Web sites have links to other sites or have affiliated subsites that contain as much or more information on the desired topic. The primary site (e.g., used the most to accomplish the targeted goal) is the one that should be evaluated with your students. If the main site and links or subsites are both heavily used, each should be evaluated separately.

You may also want to review the instrument with students to be sure that all items are clearly understood. Some educators recommend completing the instrument together one time, so students feel confident that they can then complete it on their own. We think that's a good idea because it helps support students' *expectation for success*. Once you have gone over the directions and the instrument, most students should be able to complete the instrument independently.

You as the Model

An important factor in working with and administering *WebMAC Senior* is you! If you model enthusiasm for information exploration and evaluation of information resources, you can help to spark a similar enthusiasm in your students. After all, if technology competence and information literacy are the achievement destinations, then we should help to make the journey exciting and fun! Modeling enthusiasm and showing empathy can help in achieving that goal.

Ours Is Not the Only Way

In this chapter, we have offered you some suggestions for administering the *WebMAC Senior* with students. In Chapter Twelve, you'll find reproducible overhead transparency masters and a content outline that you may want to incorporate into a lesson.

We have learned about so many creative ways that educators have used this and the other *WebMAC* instruments, and the administration procedures have varied from one instance to another. It's really up to you.

Some educators have told us that they feel the instrument is best used as part of a larger unit that integrates information literacy and the curriculum, and we agree. To make the most of this evaluation tool, it should be used after students have been exposed to evaluation as an information literacy skill. How and in what context it is used will affect how you administer *WebMAC Senior*. In Chapter Eight, you'll find a number of innovative lesson ideas that practitioners have shared with us.

COMING UP...

In Chapter Five, you will find the complete *WebMAC Senior* instrument, which is designed for use by an individual student, a small group, or an entire class. Students may use it independently or with adult guidance. Don't forget that you can also find the 24-item *WebMAC Middle* instrument and scoring grids in Appendix B. You may find this version preferable if you are working with upper middle school students or with a group of students with lower reading skills.

HIGHLIGHTS of Chapter Four

Here are some of the key points covered in Chapter Four.

▶ The different ways educators have been using *WebMAC Senior* may indicate alternative administration procedures based on the context in which the tool is used.

▶ You have a great deal of motivational influence on your learners when it comes to modeling enthusiasm for information exploration and evaluation.

▶ Perhaps the best use of *WebMAC Senior* is as part of a larger unit that integrates information literacy and the curriculum.

MINESTORMING

Are you already thinking of good ideas for using *WebMAC Senior* (or *WebMAC Middle*) with your students? Use this page to jot down any great thoughts and ideas you have minestormed from Chapter Four.

_____
_____
_____
_____
_____
_____
_____
_____
_____
_____

CHAPTER 5

WebMAC Senior

The Motivation Mining Company

Mine Map

Part I: Motivation Mining for Information Literacy

Part II: Mining Tools for Motivational Assessment

"WebMAC Senior"

Part IV: Sharing the Wealth

Part III: Panning for Web Gold

Introduction

The *WebMAC Senior* evaluation instrument contains 32 items for rating the motivational quality of a Web site. In this chapter, we present *WebMAC Senior*© (version 4.0). You are free to use it in its entirety or modify it to meet your students' needs. We recommend that you teach your students how to use *WebMAC Senior* and complete one or two evaluations together. However, there may be times when you want to be able to just hand the instrument to a student and have him or her complete it independently. Therefore, we have incorporated the entire instrument with complete directions; it is reproducible, so you have the flexibility to allow students to work independently.

Objectives

By the end of this chapter, you will be:
▶ able to implement *WebMAC Senior* with your students or allow them to complete the instrument independently.
▶ familiar with the items that comprise the *WebMAC Senior* instrument.

Using *WebMAC Senior* with High School Students

First, you will need to review the instrument's directions with your students. After you are sure students understand the directions for using *WebMAC Senior*, and if your students have had little experience using Web resources, you might want to spend a few minutes reviewing any words or terms that may be unfamiliar to them. It may be helpful to practice using the instrument once or twice before they use the instrument for the first time on their own.

On the following pages you will find the reproducible *WebMAC Senior* instrument, directions, scoring graph, and grid. *WebMAC Middle*, for grades 5-8, can be found in Appendix B.

WEBSITE MOTIVATIONAL ANALYSIS CHECKLIST SENIOR (4.0)©

Directions

Before using *WebMAC Senior*, it's a good idea to spend some time exploring the Web site to be evaluated in order to have some familiarity with its content and structure. You may need to go through the Web site at least once more to complete this checklist.

Rate your level of agreement with each of the 32 items on the next two pages by placing the appropriate number value on the line in front of each item. If you are not sure about any item, select the best response you can give.

> 3 = strongly agree
> 2 = somewhat agree
> 1 = somewhat disagree
> 0 = strongly disagree
> NA = Not Applicable

Example of completed item:

<u>3</u>   0. This Web site makes me happy.

After you have rated all 32 items, go back and look at each NA item. You should place one of the following scores next to the NA for that item.

0 = the Web site would have benefited if it had included the item (e.g., audio).
1 = the Web site didn't require that item.
2 = the Web site was better off for not including that item.

WEBSITE MOTIVATIONAL ANALYSIS CHECKLIST *WebMAC Senior (4.0)*©

Your name _____

Web site URL _____

Place the appropriate number rating for this Web site on the line preceding each item.

3 = strongly agree
2 = somewhat agree
1 = somewhat disagree
0 = strongly disagree
NA = Not Applicable

___ 1. The colors and/or background patterns used in this Web site are pleasing.
___ 2. The information at this Web site is accurate and unbiased.
___ 3. Any visual (e.g., videos, photographs) or audio information included in this Web site helps to present the topic.
___ 4. This Web site's graphics are crisp and clear.
___ 5. There is an eye-catching title or visual on the home page of this Web site.
___ 6. This Web site provides valuable links to other interesting or useful Web sites.
___ 7. I found the amount of information I needed at this Web site.
___ 8. The Web site has a "help" function that I can use at any time.
___ 9. This Web site is fun and interesting to explore.
___ 10. The Web site's information is provided by credible sources.
___ 11. There is a menu or site map at the beginning that lets me know what content is contained within the Web site.
___ 12. I can control how fast I move through this Web site at all times.
___ 13. The information included in this Web site is interesting.
___ 14. The information contained in this Web site is current and up-to-date.
___ 15. The purpose of this Web site is always clear to me.
___ 16. Navigating this Web site does not require any special skills or experience.
___ 17. The variety of formats (e.g., text, images, sound) keeps my attention.
___ 18. The information at this Web site is useful to me.
___ 19. All of the information at this Web site is presented using clear and consistent language and style.

___ 20. All of this Web site's hyperlinks are active and fully functioning.
___ 21. This Web site has novel or unique features that make it more interesting.
___ 22. This Web site provides opportunities for me to communicate with its authors.
___ 23. The text at this Web site is well-written without grammatical, spelling, or other errors.
___ 24. At all times, I can control what information at this Web site I wish to see.
___ 25. There are surprising things at this Web site.
___ 26. This Web site provides opportunities for interactivity.
___ 27. The directions for using this Web site are simple and clear.
___ 28. All buttons and other navigation mechanisms at this Web site work the way they should.
___ 29. The screen layout of this Web site is attractive.
___ 30. There is little or no unimportant or redundant information at this Web site.
___ 31. No matter where I am in this Web site, I can return to the home page or exit.
___ 32. The amount of time it takes for pictures, games, videos, and other items to appear on the screen at this Web site is reasonable.

I would visit this Web site again.   YES ☐   NO ☐

I would recommend this Web site to others.   YES ☐   NO ☐

What is the best thing about this Web site? _____

_____

_____

What needs the most improvement at this Web site? _____

_____

_____

COMING UP...

Now that you have been introduced to the *WebMAC Senior* instrument, you will want to help your students understand how to transform and understand your scores. The next two chapters will help you do that.

HIGHLIGHTS of Chapter Five

Here are some of the key points covered in Chapter Five.

▶ In order to be certain that students clearly understand the directions for using *WebMAC Senior*, spend some time reviewing unfamiliar terms and discussing the directions, and then practice filling it out.

▶ The *WebMAC Senior* instrument contains 32 statements which must be rated on a scale of "0" (strongly disagree) to "3" (strongly agree).

▶ A designation of NA is available when a particular statement does not apply to the Web site being evaluated.

MINESTORMING

As you were reviewing the items that comprise *WebMAC Senior*, did you think of ways you might incorporate the instrument into your school's information literacy curriculum? Why not do some *minestorming* right now! Use the space below to record the ideas you got from Chapter Five.

_____
_____
_____
_____
_____
_____
_____
_____
_____

CHAPTER 6

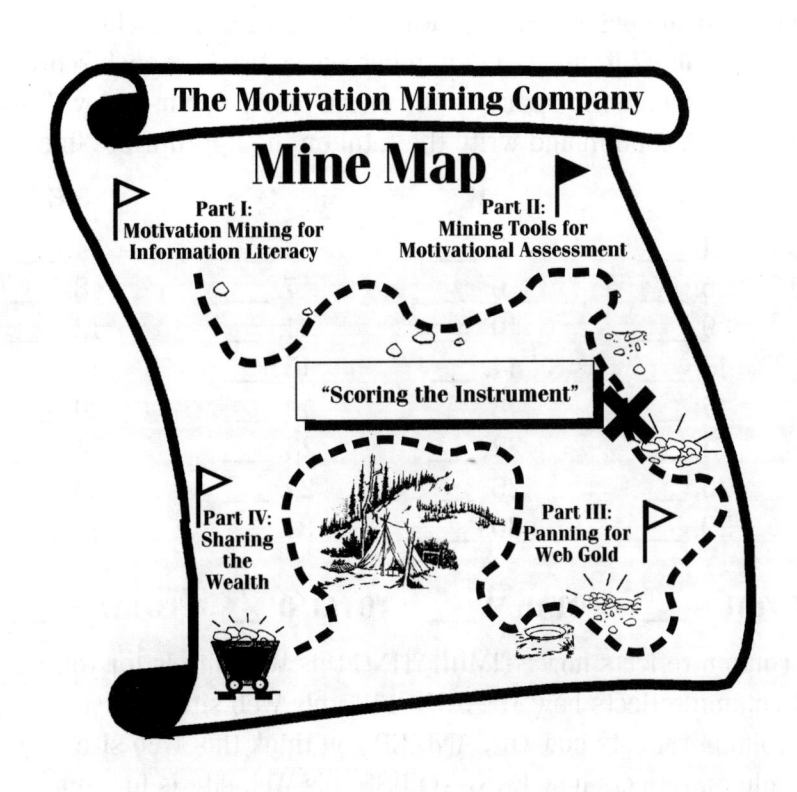

Scoring the Instrument

The Motivation Mining Company

Mine Map

Part I: Motivation Mining for Information Literacy

Part II: Mining Tools for Motivational Assessment

"Scoring the Instrument"

Part IV: Sharing the Wealth

Part III: Panning for Web Gold

Introduction

In this chapter, you will find everything you need to teach your students how to score *WebMAC Senior*, including tally sheets and a grid for charting results. Full explanations of scores are provided in Chapter Seven.

Objectives

When you have completed Chapter Six, you will be able to:
▶ plot and total item scores in a four **attribute** graph.
▶ use the individual and class tally forms.
▶ use the grids to visually represent evaluation results.

Scoring *WebMAC Senior*

Before transferring scores, students go back to each item designated "NA" and choose a score for that item based on the following criteria:

■ 0 points if you feel that the site would have benefited if it had included the item (e.g., audio).
■ 1 point if you feel that the Web site didn't require that item.
■ 2 points if you believe the site was better off for not including that item.

When all 32 items have a number score, transfer each score into the appropriately numbered space in one of the four columns below. Then add the scores for each column and write the total on the appropriate line.

S	**M**	**O**	**E**
1. ___	2. ___	3. ___	4. ___
5. ___	6. ___	7. ___	8. ___
9. ___	10. ___	11. ___	12. ___
13. ___	14. ___	15. ___	16. ___
17. ___	18. ___	19. ___	20. ___
21. ___	22. ___	23. ___	24. ___
25. ___	26. ___	27. ___	28. ___
29. ___	30. ___	31. ___	32. ___
TOTAL S ___	TOTAL M ___	TOTAL O ___	TOTAL E ___

The **S** column reflects how STIMULATING this Web site is for you.
The **M** column reflects how MEANINGFUL this Web site is to you.
The **O** column reflects how ORGANIZED you think this Web site is.
The **E** column reflects how EASY TO USE this Web site is for you.

Transforming Scores

Now you may transform your scores into visual representations so that you can clearly see the results of your evaluation. First, take each of the four total scores above and plot them (either with a dot or a bar) on the graph below. If you use dots, connect the dots to make a line. Information on interpreting your scores is provided in Chapter Seven.

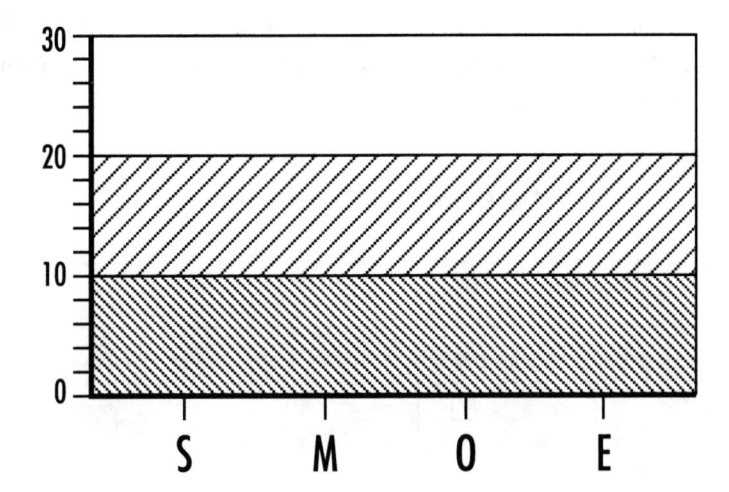

Next, take the total scores from the four **attributes** (S, M, O, E) and add them together in the following way to get your two overall motivational quality scores.

$$S + M = \underline{} \text{ (V)} \qquad O + E = \underline{} \text{ (XS)}$$

The **V** score reflects a summary motivation score on the Value dimension; i.e. how much that Web site provides value and is engaging and useful. The **XS** score reflects a summary motivation score on the Expectation for Success dimension; that is, how organized and easy to use the Web site is.

Plotting the Scores

Once you have transformed scores into two overall motivational quality scores, you can plot your scores on the scoring grid below. Place a dot for the **V** score along the Value continuum and a dot for the **XS** score along the Expectation for Success continuum on the grid. Next, draw straight lines to their intersection point, which represents the overall motivational quality score of the Web site. We provide an example below. In this example the evaluated Web site received a Value score of 40 and an Expectation for Success score of 18. Their intersection point falls within the lower right quadrant of the grid.

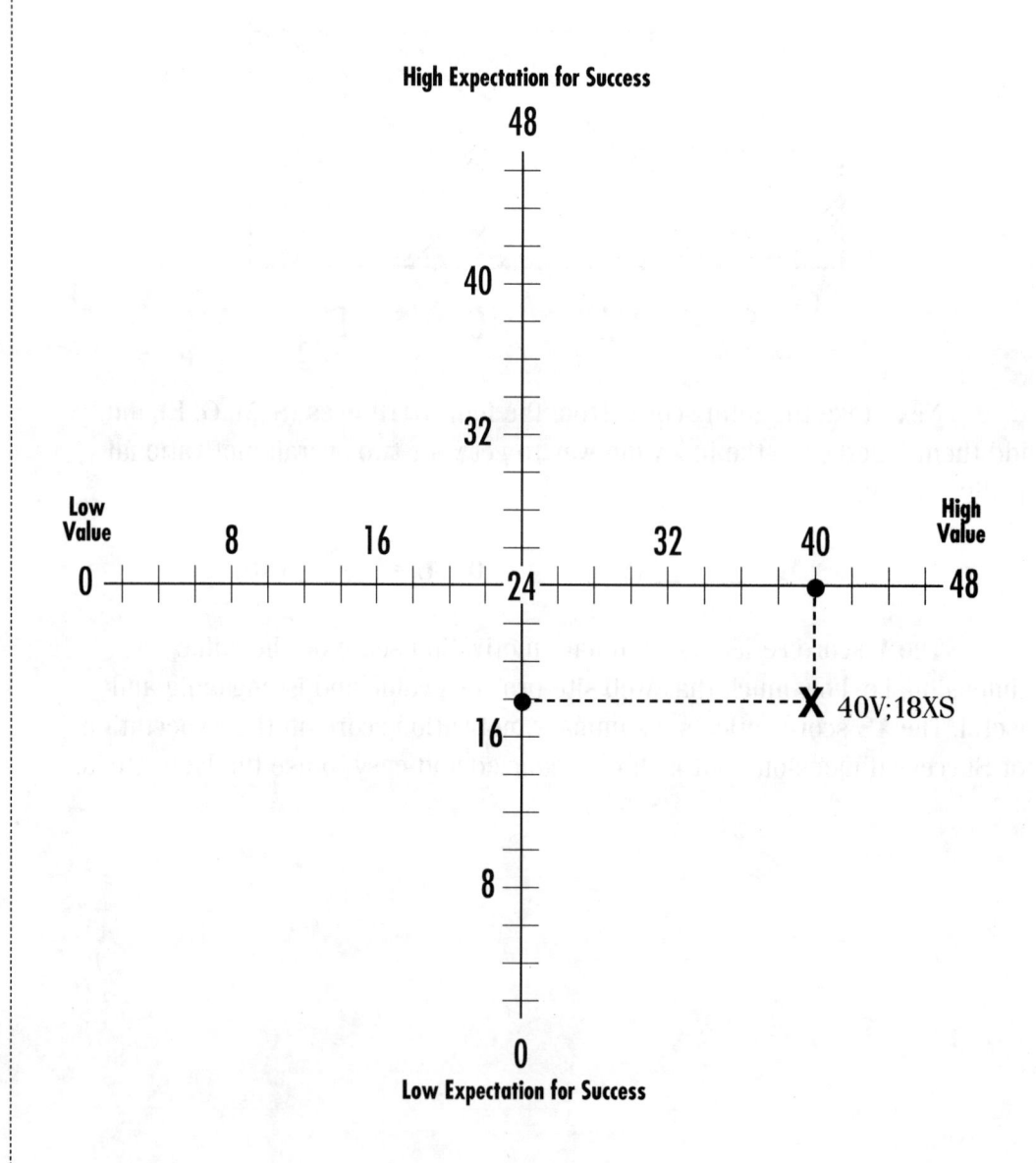

High Expectation for Success

48

40

32

| Low Value | 8 | 16 | | 32 | 40 | High Value |

0 — — — — — — — — — — — — 24 — — — — — — — — — — — — 48

● – – – – – – – – – – – – **X** 40V;18XS

16

8

0

Low Expectation for Success

Rating the Web Site (Individual)

Now it's time for your students to record actual scores from their Web site evaluation onto the scoring grid. Each student plots the score for **V** along the Value continuum and the score for **XS** along the Expectation for Success continuum. Then, the student draws straight lines to the intersection point.

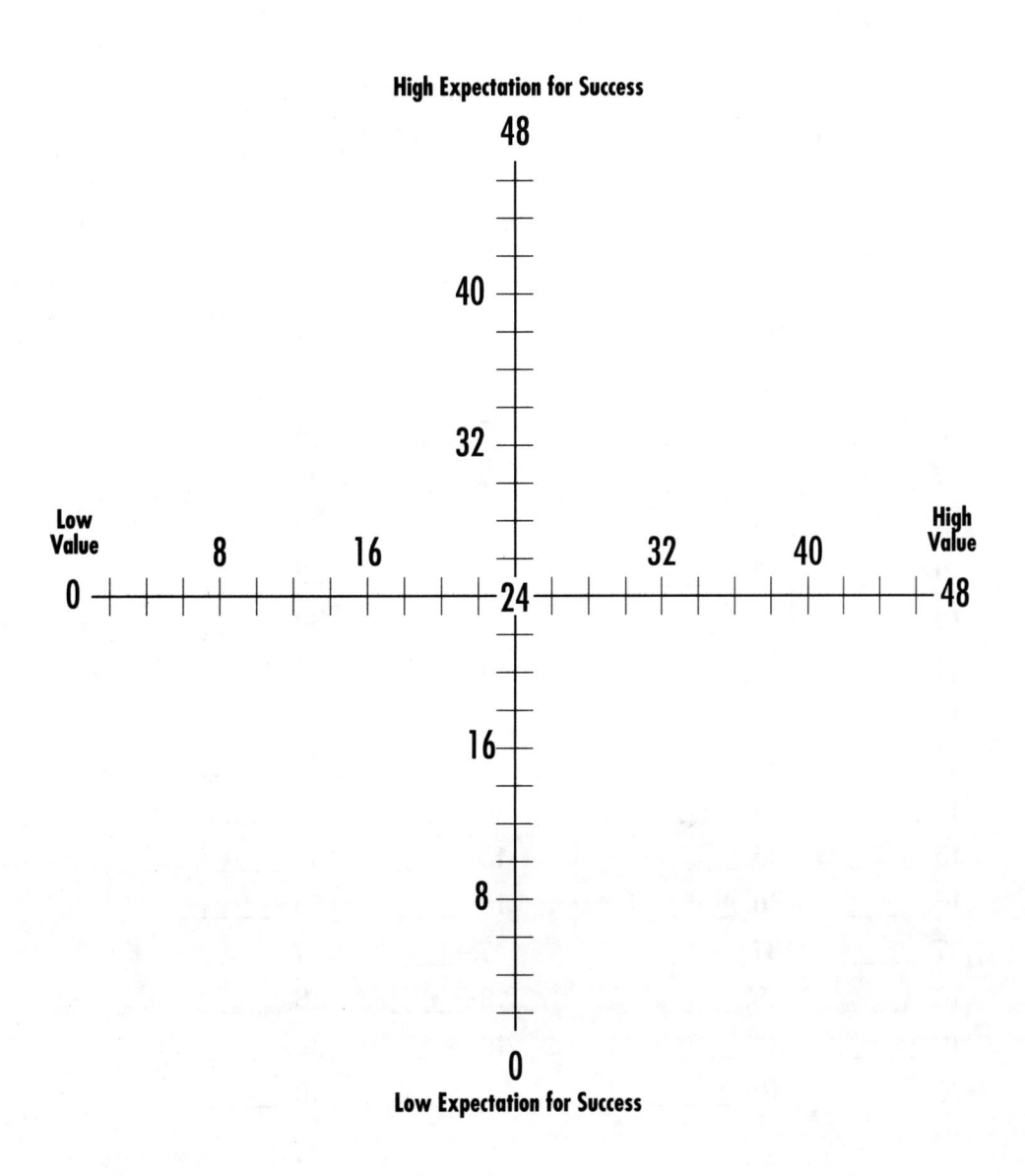

High Expectation for Success

48

40

32

Low Value 0 —— 8 —— 16 —— 24 —— 32 —— 40 —— 48 **High Value**

16

8

0

Low Expectation for Success

Class Tally

Sometimes a group or entire class will evaluate the same Web site. If you would like to calculate their summary and average scores, you can use the tally sheet below to record each individual student's scores (up to 40 students) for **V** and **XS** on the columns. Then total and average each column and plot the class average scores on the scoring grid on the next page.

Individual Totals		**Individual Totals**	
V Scores		**XS Scores**	
1. _____	21. _____	1. _____	21. _____
2. _____	22. _____	2. _____	22. _____
3. _____	23. _____	3. _____	23. _____
4. _____	24. _____	4. _____	24. _____
5. _____	25. _____	5. _____	25. _____
6. _____	26. _____	6. _____	26. _____
7. _____	27. _____	7. _____	27. _____
8. _____	28. _____	8. _____	28. _____
9. _____	29. _____	9. _____	29. _____
10. _____	30. _____	10. _____	30. _____
11. _____	31. _____	11. _____	31. _____
12. _____	32. _____	12. _____	32. _____
13. _____	33. _____	13. _____	33. _____
14. _____	34. _____	14. _____	34. _____
15. _____	35. _____	15. _____	35. _____
16. _____	36. _____	16. _____	36. _____
17. _____	37. _____	17. _____	37. _____
18. _____	38. _____	18. _____	38. _____
19. _____	39. _____	19. _____	39. _____
20. _____	40. _____	20. _____	40. _____

TOTAL V Scores _____

Average V Score _____

TOTAL XS Scores _____

Average XS Score _____

Rating the Web Site (Class)

Visually represent the results of the class tally sheet by plotting the class Average **V** Score and the class Average **XS** score on the grid below. Then draw straight lines to their intersection point. The intersection point represents the class overall motivation quality rating.

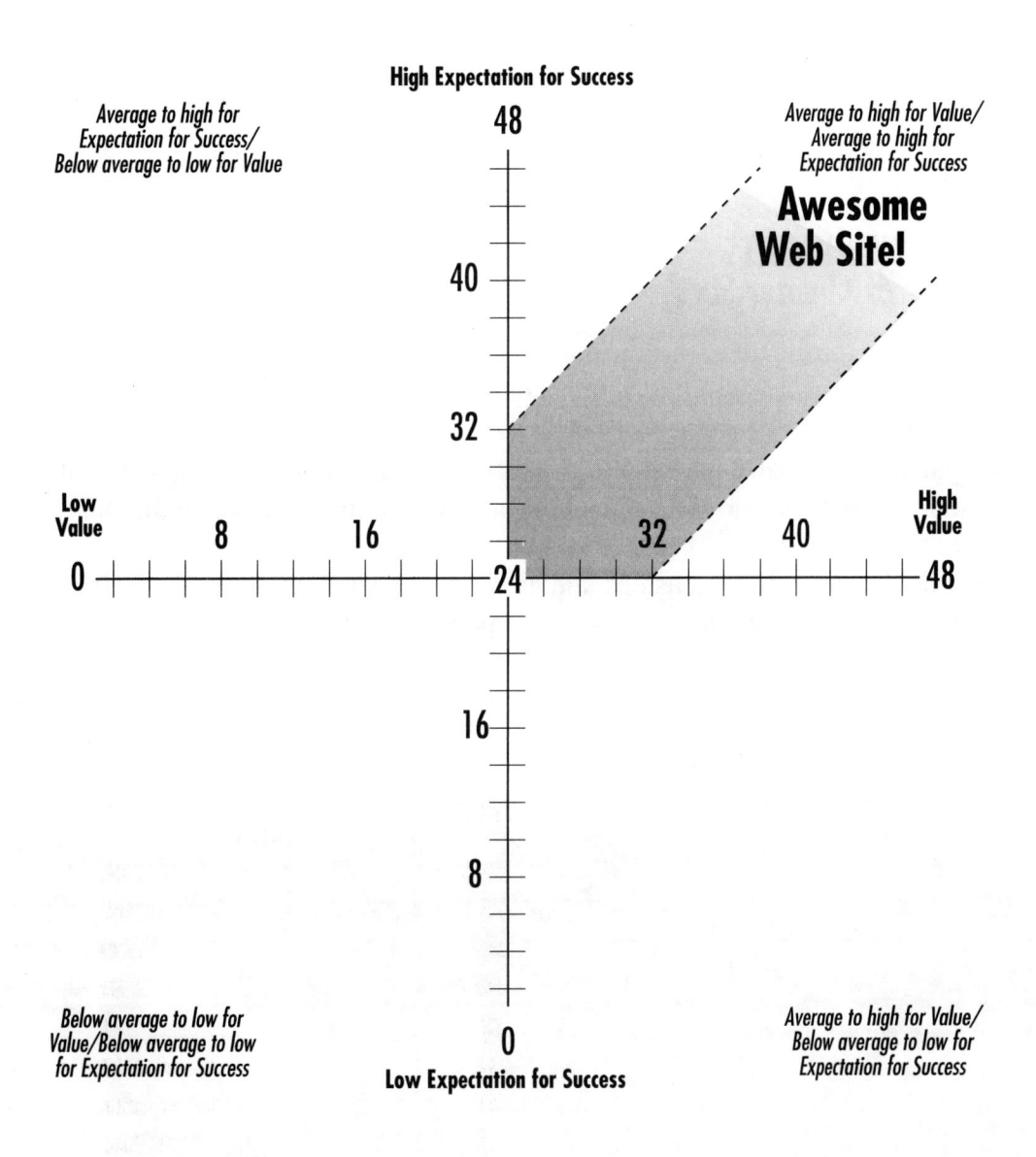

High Expectation for Success

Average to high for Expectation for Success/ Below average to low for Value

Average to high for Value/ Average to high for Expectation for Success

Awesome Web Site!

Low Value 0 — 8 — 16 — 24 — 32 — 40 — 48 **High Value**

48 — 40 — 32 — 16 — 8 — 0

Below average to low for Value/Below average to low for Expectation for Success

Average to high for Value/ Below average to low for Expectation for Success

Low Expectation for Success

COMING UP...

What do your scores mean? How can you use your scores to make recommendations for improvement of a Web site? You'll find out how to interpret your scores in Chapter Seven.

HIGHLIGHTS of Chapter Six

Here are some of the key points covered in Chapter Six.

▶ *WebMAC Senior's* two motivational quality dimensions are *Value* and *Expectation for Success*.

▶ Value can be broken down into two attributes: Stimulating and Meaningful. Expectation for Success can be broken down into two attributes: Organized and Easy to Use.

▶ *WebMAC Senior's* dimensions and attributes may be represented visually (for individuals and for groups) on graphs and grids.

MINESTORMING

As you were transforming your scores and plotting them on the grid provided in Chapter Six, you may have guessed what your scores mean. Use this page to jot down your ideas. Then compare your ideas with the information on interpretation of scores in Chapter Seven.

_____
_____
_____
_____
_____
_____
_____
_____
_____
_____

CHAPTER 7

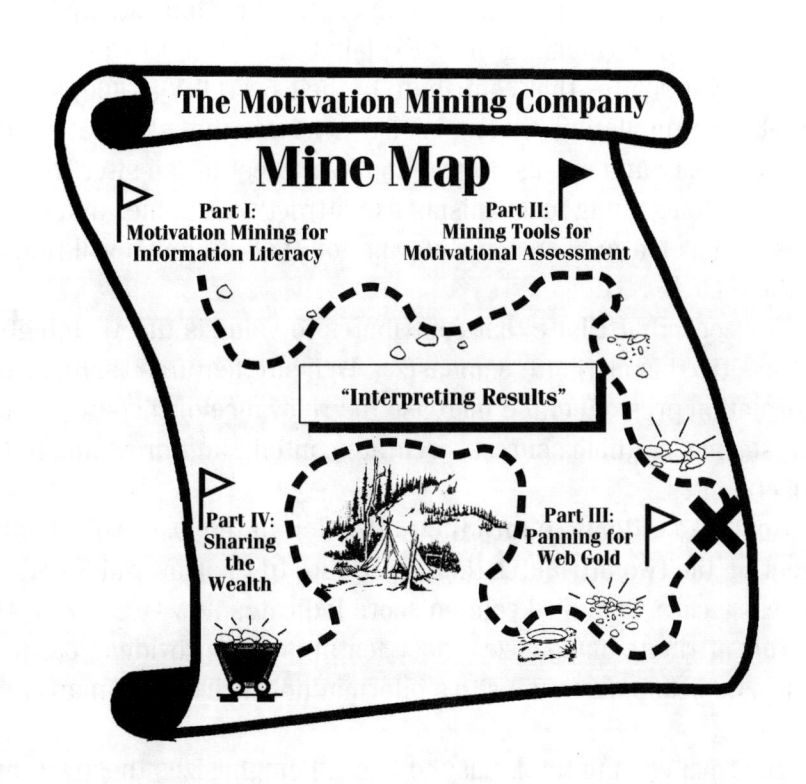

Interpreting Results

The Motivation Mining Company
Mine Map

Part I: Motivation Mining for Information Literacy

Part II: Mining Tools for Motivational Assessment

"Interpreting Results"

Part IV: Sharing the Wealth

Part III: Panning for Web Gold

Introduction

Once students have explored how evaluation applies to Web resources and completed *WebMAC Senior* with at least one Web site, they are likely to begin asking what their scores mean. Interpreting scores can be the culminating activity for a unit on evaluation. In this chapter, we describe how to interpret individual and class scores.

Objectives

By the end of Chapter Seven, you will be able to:
- model the process of interpreting scores to your students.
- analyze the four attribute scores.
- pinpoint any trouble spots in order to revise and improve the Web site.
- interpret the **V** and **XS** dimension scores.
- interpret overall motivational quality.
- discuss summary results with your students.

Interpreting Scores for the Four Attributes

Let's begin by helping students interpret their four attribute scores, that is, the four total column scores. Explain that the first two column scores represent the attributes that contribute to their overall **V** (Value) score. The first attribute, Stimulating (**S**), emphasizes features that stimulate and maintain curiosity and engage the student's interest in the site. These features include attention-gaining mechanisms like attractive graphics and pleasing colors as well as features such as information that student's will find interesting.

The second attribute that contributes to Value is the Meaningfulness (**M**) of the site. This attribute emphasizes Web site features that add value to the information presented and increase the relevance of the site to the student, such as credible sources, accurate content, and providing links to other useful sites.

Now ask students to turn their attention to the last two column totals representing the two attributes that contribute to their overall **XS** (Expectation for Success) score. The third column score indicates how Organized (**O**) the site is. This attribute emphasizes those features that provide a logical overall structure and sequence to the site's information, such as site maps and clear directions.

The final column total, Easy to Use (**E**) emphasizes those features that affect students' confidence in their ability to successfully navigate the Web site and find the information they need. Examples are control mechanisms and reasonable loading time for graphics and other visuals.

To understand these four numerical scores, display the graph below. Explain that a perfect total score for each of the attributes is 24. A score of 16 or higher indicates that the Web site is already highly motivating for that attribute. If the attribute received a score of 8-15, it requires some improvement, while a score of less than 8 means the Web site needs serious attention and revision. Most Web sites will need improvement in at least one attribute area. Most "Awesome Web Sites" will have high scores for all four attributes.

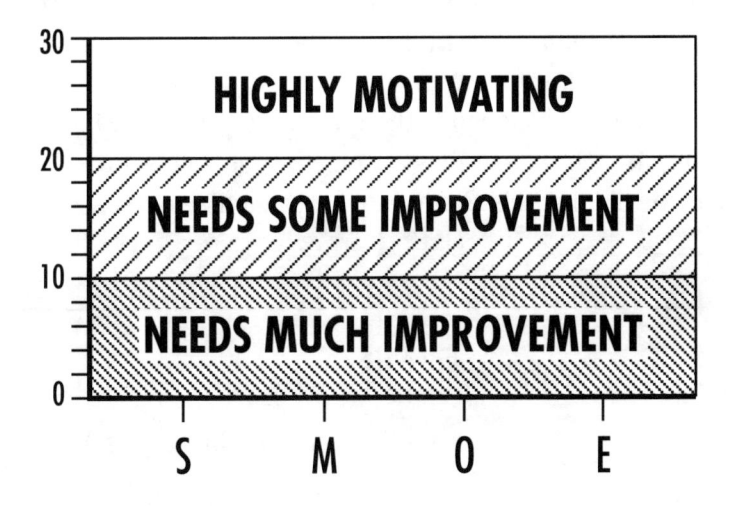

```
30 ┌─────────────────────────┐
   │                         │
   │   HIGHLY MOTIVATING     │
20 │─────────────────────────│
   │   NEEDS SOME IMPROVEMENT│
10 │─────────────────────────│
   │   NEEDS MUCH IMPROVEMENT│
 0 └─────────────────────────┘
       S      M      O      E
```

Pinpointing Trouble Spots

If you or your students are trying to improve your own Web site or are recommending areas of improvement to another Web designer, you will want to be able to pinpoint precise trouble spots in order to correct them and help to raise a particular attribute's score. This requires an item analysis. Here's an easy way to do it.

Scan down the scores on the *WebMAC Senior* instrument. Circle any item that received a score of **0** or **1**. Then find all items that were scored **NA** and circle only those that were later scored **0**. You have just identified the features *most in need of improvement*. Now refer back to each of the items, thoroughly reviewing your Web site to see which features you might want to revise or add.

Don't worry if you can't fix every feature—remember you are aiming for an attribute score of **20** or higher. This does not require *all* features to be rated highly, and they probably can't or shouldn't be for some Web sites. Although you want to have a Web site with an high overall motivational quality score, you don't want to add features that are inappropriate or superfluous. You (and your students) are the judges of what features are most important for your Web site.

Explaining the Significance of the V and XS Scores

Now that you understand how to interpret the scores for the four attributes, let's look at the overall Value and Expectation for Success scores that contribute to a student's overall perception of a Web site. Once your students have transformed their four attribute scores into two scores representing **V** and **XS**, you could review some of the features that contribute to making that Web site valuable to them and the features that make them feel that they can be successful at that Web site.

To help your students interpret their **V** and **XS** scores, we have developed a Scoring Key that describes a range of possible scores. You might want to reproduce or display this Score Key for students to use, so it appears below.

Score Key

V (*Value*)		**XS** (*Expectation for Success*)	
0-11	Poor	0-11	Poor
12-23	Below Average	12-23	Below Average
24-31	Average	24-31	Average
32-39	Good	32-39	Good
40-48	Excellent	40-48	Excellent

Interpreting Your Overall Motivational Quality Rating

Now that students understand the significance of each score, you can discuss how the two scores together contribute to the overall rating of the Web site. An excellent site does well on both scores. You can make this idea more concrete by asking questions like the following and leaving enough time in between to get thoughtful responses from your students:

> *What if you found a Web site that had lots of interesting information that you could use for a project you were working on, but it wasn't easy to find that information on the Web site and everything took a real long time to get to, how would you*

feel? (Possible answers: angry, frustrated, give up) Why?

What if you found a Web site that made it easy to find the information, but you were unsure how current the information was or who the source of the information was, how would you feel? (Possible answers: confused, uneasy) Why?

Do you think you would stay at either of those Web sites for very long if you couldn't get what you needed, or if you were unsure about the information you found there? Why or why not?

How many of you would come back and visit that site again some time? Why or why not?

These types of questions help students understand the importance of high motivational quality for the Web sites they encounter.

If you have completed the class tally and grid, you may also want to help students interpret those results. This helps demonstrate to students that often it takes the work of a number of evaluators to make decisions when considering modifications or changes to Web sites. It also illustrates how different evaluators may make different judgments about the same Web site. Using the class tally and then plotting the average class score helps students to see how their individual input contributes to the larger evaluation.

Plotting the scores for the two dimensions on the grid helps to illustrate how it takes *good* scores in both Value and Expectation for Success to have a Web site with high motivational quality. Once students have determined the intersection point for their V and XS scores, point out that that point falls into one of four quadrants on the grid. Scores can be visualized by plotting them on the grid on the next page.

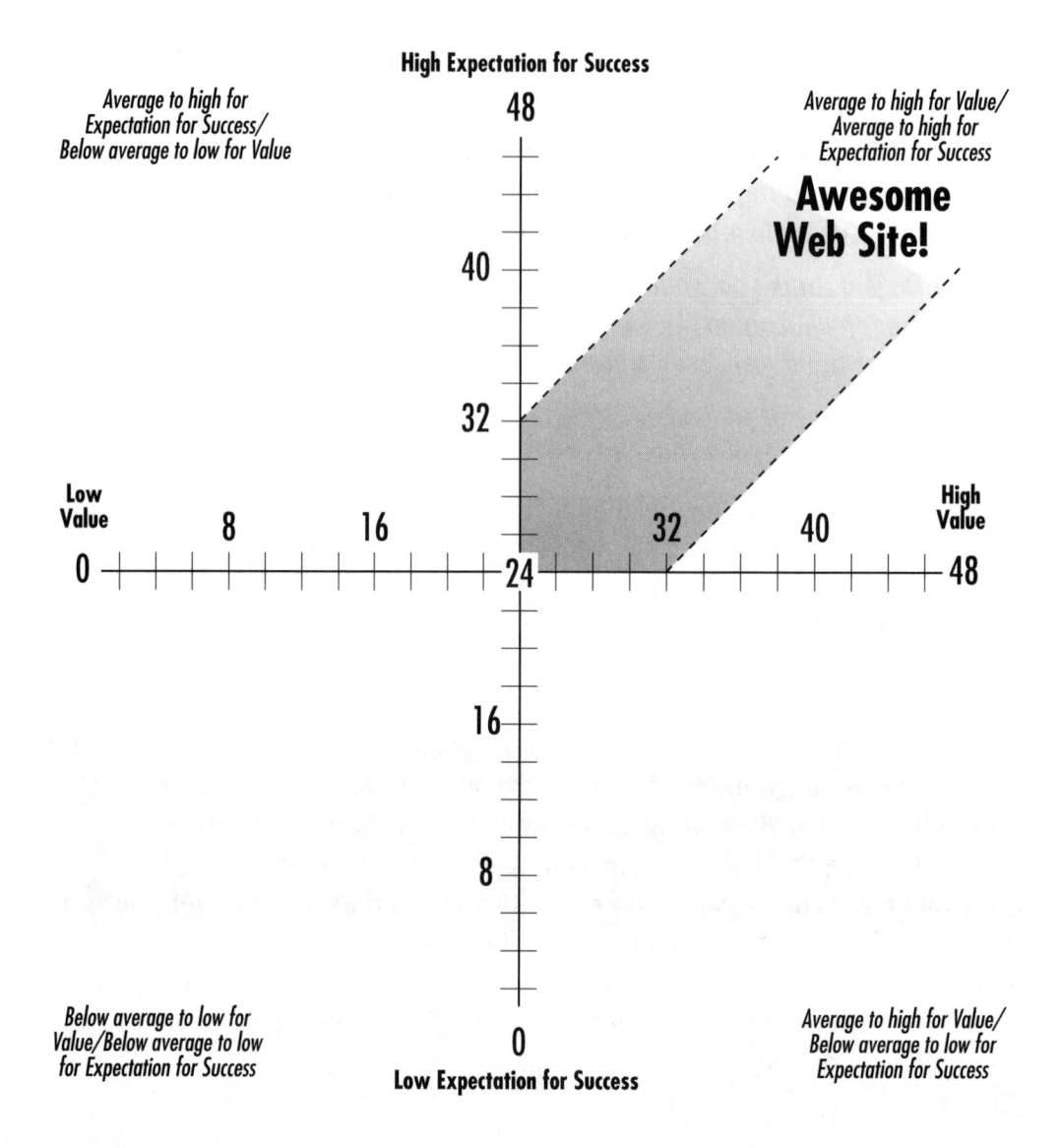

Average to high for Expectation for Success / Below average to low for Value

High Expectation for Success

Average to high for Value / Average to high for Expectation for Success

Awesome Web Site!

Low Value — 0, 8, 16, 24, 32, 40, 48 — **High Value**

Below average to low for Value / Below average to low for Expectation for Success

Low Expectation for Success

Average to high for Value / Below average to low for Expectation for Success

Awesome Web Sites

Explain that only sites with scores of 40 or better for both V and XS would have an intersection point that falls into the *Awesome Web Site* range. Although an "Awesome Web Site" is one that scores generally high in all areas, it is important to explain that no Web site is perfect. There are always areas in need of some improvement. Identifying low scoring items (as we recommend in the section on "Pinpointing Trouble Spots") provides information about these areas.

Furthermore, a Web site does not have to include "bells and whistles" to be rated *Awesome*. For example, animations may or may not add to the motivational quality of a specific site. So-called "glitz" is not an essential criterion for a Web site to receive an Awesome rating.

Once your students have identified an *Awesome Web Site*, they may want to nominate it for our Awesome Web Site Award (AWArd). You can find out how to do that in the final chapter of this book.

COMING UP...

Many educators from across the country and beyond have already put *WebMAC Senior* and *WebMAC Middle* into action. In Chapter Eight, we present the results of interviews we conducted with teachers and library media specialists who described how they are making motivation mining the Web work for them.

HIGHLIGHTS of Chapter Seven

Here are some of the key points covered in Chapter Seven.

▶ Students can interpret their scores on the four motivation attributes, the two motivation dimensions, or overall motivational quality.

▶ Plotting scores on a grid helps students to visually interpret the results of their Web evaluations and to compare scores of individuals and classes.

▶ Excellent Web sites have high scores for both Value *and* Expectation for Success.

▶ An item analysis using *WebMAC Senior* can help you and your students pinpoint the trouble spots so you can improve your own Web site.

MINESTORMING

Before moving on to read how some of your colleagues are using Web-based resources to teach evaluation skills, take a moment, think about what you have learned in Chapter Seven, and minestorm some of your own ideas for teaching this important information skill.

_____
_____
_____
_____
_____
_____
_____
_____
_____
_____

PART III

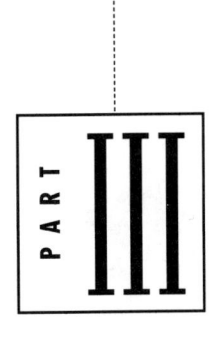

Panning for Web Gold: Making Motivation Mining Work for You

CHAPTER 8

A Treasure Trove of Ideas from Educators

Introduction

Evaluating a Web site is a meaningful and enjoyable activity that gives students the opportunity to develop an important critical thinking skill. Instruments like *WebMAC Senior* provide an exciting opportunity for library media specialists and teachers to work together to plan and teach curriculum-integrated lessons that promote evaluation and information literacy.

In preparing this book, we interviewed a number of educators to get their ideas on evaluation of Web resources and the importance of motivation. We also wanted to hear their insights regarding the use of *WebMAC Senior* (and *WebMAC Middle*) with students. They not only described the context in which they have already used *WebMAC Senior* but also shared with us some ideas for how they might use it in the future.

You will also find that the amount of time educators allocated for teaching students about *WebMAC Senior* ranged from a single teaching episode to incorporating it as part of a week or even month-long, research project. Many practitioners have also told us that once students have used the *WebMAC* instrument one or two times, they seem to internalize it to a level where they automatically apply many of the items every time they visit the Web—even when they do not have the instrument!

Throughout this book, we have used the "mining" analogy with reference to motivation. It's fun and interesting to contrast such an old art with such new technology as the World Wide Web. Just as in "the ole days," using appropriate tools can help you to know if you've struck Web gold. In this chapter, we share some of the precious "gems" provided by teachers and library media specialists in order to illustrate *WebMAC Senior* in action. We also sprinkle in some of our own "nuggets," our ideas for using *WebMAC Senior*. We hope these gems and nuggets will trigger some wonderful ideas of your own.

Objectives

At the end of this chapter you will be:
▶ aware of some ways your colleagues are using *WebMAC Senior* with their students.
▶ able to generate some ideas for how you could use *WebMAC Senior* (or *WebMAC Middle*) in your school.

Gems and Nuggets from the "MasterMines"

Kathy Schrock believes that the best way to teach critical Web evaluation skills is integrated with "real" assignments and projects.[1] We agree, so we asked some middle and high school teachers and library media specialists to describe how they taught their students to use *WebMAC Senior* to find Web treasures. Many of them told us how they collaborated to teach Web evaluation skills, integrated with students' assignments and projects. Here are some of their "gems" (and some of our idea nuggets) and accounts of what they did and how they did it. We've also included a couple of their actual lesson plans (which you may want to use or adapt) in Appendix A.

NUGGET: Have students write an assessment of your school's (or library's or classroom's) Web site and provide a report of constructive ideas for improvement.

Our first gem comes in the form of a unit planned jointly by Nancy Nicholson, library media specialist, and Michael Charbonneau, 12th grade journalism teacher from Mexico (New York) High School. Nancy and Michael collaborated on a lesson using *WebMAC Senior* with a group of 35 12th graders. When we asked them why they thought evaluating Web sites was important, Nancy stated, "Kids think the Internet is the 'be-all, end-all.' Often it's the first place they go to find information. We find so many students who think that anything they find on the Web is absolute truth, and they don't have the skills to be able to evaluate whether it's valuable or not. Evaluation is something we teach more and more." Michael added, "I just started using the Web about a year ago. Judging Web sites was something I had never thought about. Now I realize that both students and teachers need to be more critical about what we're using as sources of information."

Nancy believes both verifiable content and motivational aspects are important when assessing Web sites. "We want students to know whether [or not] the information they find is coming from good sources, but it's also got to be interesting for them and they must have easy access," she said. "Otherwise, they won't spend much time there." Nancy's right. No matter how good the content is, if the site doesn't have high motivational quality, it is less likely to engage and maintain the students' interest.

How did Nancy and Michael decide to work together to help students learn to critically evaluate Web sites? Nancy recounted the circumstances, "Michael and I had been discussing the issue of kids and the Internet and how they're drawn to it for research. We agreed they needed some guidelines for using it. Our district is in the midst of a technology plan, and we're getting more and more technology throughout the school. Students need to know what's there. More than that, they need instruction to know how to find what's 'good.'"

We hear from so many educators that their school or district is undergoing major technology initiatives. In most cases, Internet access is available for the first time to teachers and students. While this is a time of great excitement and opportunity, it also can result in substantial changes in the way teachers teach and students learn. The learning task that Michael assigned to his students as part of a unit on "propaganda" reflect some of those changes.

The 35 high school journalism students were required to find information on the Web about author George Orwell. (Michael chose Orwell because they had read several of his works.) The students then had to use *WebMAC Senior* to evaluate one of the Web sites they found. "When I explained what we were going to do, evaluate Web sites, they had no idea what I was talking about," Michael said. "After they looked at the criteria, they realized just how much goes into a Web site to make it reliable and attractive."

We asked the dynamic duo how their students reacted to using the *WebMAC* instrument. Nancy commented, "The students liked using *WebMAC Senior*. They thought it was a very useful tool that gave them insight into what makes a good Web site. As they worked, they were very intent and [focused]. They seemed excited about what they were finding." Michael added, "They didn't look at *WebMAC Senior* as a 'homework ditto.' It was something different. The 40 items captured their attention. He said some of the students were surprised to see how many different items could be used to judge a Web site. "They were investigative... they were thoughtful... and they enjoyed the task! The instrument was extremely easy to use."

Nancy and Michael envision *WebMAC Senior* in other ways with high school students in the future. "We are in the process of converting our school newspaper, *The Talkative*, from paper-based to Internet-based in order to reach a broader audience (e.g., alumni, community members). I like to think that having their work on the Web for all to see puts more emphasis on quality, and the students do a better job," Michael explained. Nancy added that their school newspaper is now located on a commercial Web site, and many students have reacted negatively to the way the site looks (all text, no graphics). "They find it very boring to look at," Nancy commented. We would guess that this Web site wouldn't get high scores if evaluated with *WebMAC Senior*!

Currently, plans are underway for students to design their own school newspaper site and link it to their existing school site. Nancy and Michael could use *WebMAC Senior* in two ways here. They could use it as a design tool, providing guidelines for student developers as to what features the site should include and how it should look and work. They could also teach some of the non-journalism students to use *WebMAC Senior*, and ask them to critically evaluate their school newspaper site and provide feedback or suggestions for improvement to the student developers. The nice thing about Web sites is that they can be changed and updated relatively easily.

Michael described another project for which *WebMAC Senior* would be appropriate. "Next year we are going to involve students in a year-long project we are calling 'Senior Quest.' Their preliminary work will be to research a topic of their choice (for example, an adopted student may want to research adoption procedures and practices). This is a hands-on project where some students may create their own Web sites. I hope they will take the criteria and use it as an outline. They'll want to get as many hits as possible. *WebMAC Senior* gives them all of the criteria to attract and hold people at their site. Using the *WebMAC Senior* tool would be a neat way to get kids involved."

Nancy also plans to use *WebMAC Senior* in the fall with incoming freshmen in the context of Freshman Orientation. She told us, "We're in the process of creating a student research manual, and a large part of that is on searching Web sites. We're trying to emphasize critical evaluation in this manual. These students haven't had much access to the Internet in middle school, so this is a wonderful opportunity to teach them the skills from the very beginning. I think *WebMAC Senior* would be a very good tool for them as they learn to use the Internet."

But students are not the only ones in Nancy's plan for the future. "I think this will be a helpful tool for our teachers, too, because we are providing a lot of Internet training to them. They could use *WebMAC Senior* to choose Web sites for their teaching. Even if some teachers are connected at home and have some experience using the Internet, they still need evaluation skills, just to be able to tell trash from treasure."

Nancy's point is a good one. Sometimes we focus so much on helping students become information literate that we forget that some teachers may need to learn the same critical evaluation skills for choosing Web sites to use in their lessons. That's why we included all the materials you need to provide an inservice workshop for your colleagues. (You'll find them in Chapter Eleven.)

As we ended our interview Michael stated, "I would use *WebMAC Senior* again. It will be one of the first things I'll do with the Senior Quest project." Nancy ended by commenting, "I think it has been a very good experience. Now even I have started to look at Web sites a little more [discerningly]!"

NUGGET — Stimulate class discussions that explore the differences between evaluating networked electronic resources and print resources. Then, have the class create a list of the "Top Ten Features" to address when evaluating all resources and display it in the library media center and classroom.

Our next gem comes from Marilyn G. Natke, library media specialist at Chittenango (New York) Middle School. The idea for her lesson first came from the sixth grade computer teachers who wanted their students to learn to evaluate Web sites. Marilyn told us, "One of the teachers had a tool that was very content-oriented. Then I showed them the *WebMAC* instrument, where content is part of it but it focuses on motivation. They looked at it and thought it was very good, and said, 'Let's go with this one. It ties in both.'

"Unfortunately, the teachers soon found they couldn't use the instrument with their classes because their computers are not hooked up to a direct T1 line, therefore only two or three students [could] access the Internet simultaneously. Once this problem is resolved, I definitely see the computer teachers and I working together to use [the instrument] with whole classes."

This temporary glitch didn't stop Marilyn. She decided to use *WebMAC Middle* with the 40-plus members of her Library Club (grades 6-8). These are students who want to go one step beyond what the other students do in the library. She started with one of the officers of the club, an eighth grader we'll call "Jay." Marilyn thinks it's important for her students to learn to evaluate Web sites because she finds they are using the Web at home as well as in school. She said, "[There is] lot of great stuff and a lot of terrible stuff out there. As educators, we need to help kids learn ways of sifting through that and finding the best that's out there instead of the mediocre."

Marilyn reviewed *WebMAC Middle's* administration directions thoroughly, and then used parts of it with Jay. She said, "The first time, we did the scoring and transformed the scores together. This helped to build [Jay's] confidence in his ability to do the task. Although the instrument seemed a bit overwhelming to [Jay] at first, it turned out to be quicker and easier than he thought." Marilyn said he really enjoyed using it.

At first, Marilyn was worried that if a Web site was not very "glitzy," Jay wouldn't rate it very highly. She thought as a librarian *she* was able to judge if a site was great, but she wasn't sure what the student would think. She was pleased to see that when Jay actually completed the instrument, he discovered that if you are successful in using a site and if you find the information you want, that's what makes it motivating. "When [Jay] graphs

[Web sites], a lot of the sites are now in the "Awesome Web Site" category, not because they have all sorts of graphics and exciting things necessarily but because they are really a good reference tools." Marilyn was very surprised at this outcome, and so was Jay!

"My plan was to ask the Library Club to help me find some good author resources on the Web. There are all these different Web sites on this topic, but I wasn't sure which ones to bookmark for students to use. So I asked Jay to go through and find two of the best ones to recommend," Marilyn said. She and Jay sat down and looked at the Web site together and went over the instrument's questions. "At first," Marilyn said, "[Jay] thought a lot of the items were [Not Applicable], so we talked more about it and found that, although there were a couple of NA's, he was able to score most of them. He hadn't clicked on to all of the hyperlinks and really dug deeply into the Web site, so he had to go back and thoroughly look at the entire Web site." Marilyn's experience reinforces our recommendation that students spend some time exploring the Web site before completing the checklist.

Marilyn really enjoyed using the instrument with Jay. She can't wait to introduce *WebMAC Middle* to the other members of the Library Club. She also had some great ideas about how teachers and library media specialists could use the evaluation tool. "I think this instrument would be valuable for teachers to use the instrument to evaluate Web sites for bookmarking and Web whacking," Marilyn said. "They could find sites that they would recommend, even to their colleagues. We have 10 sixth grade teachers, and if they were to evaluate and find the best Web sites on different topics and share what they find with their colleagues, it would be great." Another idea she had was for the librarians in her school library system to evaluate Web sites and share the best ones with each other. Marilyn also believes the *WebMAC* instruments are tools library media specialists can use to achieve "their goal as instructional leaders to help students and teachers learn how to use the Internet and Web sites in a much more effective way."

NUGGET

When assigning students research projects where they have to gather information from a variety of information resources (including Web sites), require them to evaluate their Web sites using *WebMAC Senior* and include written summaries of their evaluations with their projects.

Maryann Mazzaferro, library media specialist at Oriskany (New York) Central School, collaborated with Lisa Mlynarski, the music teacher, to use with a small group of eighth graders. Maryann told us, "Nowadays, with so much information out on the Internet and not really knowing the quality of the material you come across, evaluation becomes extremely important, especially with junior and senior high school students." She said she thought *WebMAC Senior* was an effective instrument because it identified the sites that are applicable to the work that students are doing and they get satisfaction from it.

After planning the lesson together, Lisa brought the students into the library to use a Web site on rock stars that she and Maryann had chosen for the students. This assignment was highly relevant to the students because many of the rock stars discussed on the Web site would be coming for the Woodstock concert, which is held just a few miles from their community. That made the assignment fun and very relevant because many of the students were planning to go to the concert.

After the students completed the instrument, they plotted the scores and discovered that all of them had rated the site an *Awesome Web Site*. Maryann was really pleased with the results of this lesson. "Once the kids got into using the instrument and realized the value of using it, they absolutely loved it. They felt empowered—as though they had taken part in the lesson." she said. "We hear this a lot from teachers and library media specialists. Having the skills and tools to evaluate the information they find and the information resources they use gives students a sense of empowerment that they can have some control over their learning. This is the first step to becoming self-directed, independent learners.

Now Lisa and Maryann are planning a different lesson to use with an entire class using *WebMAC Senior*! We'll be sure to check back with them to find out how the lesson goes and report the results on our Web site at www.MotivationMining.com.

NUGGET

Sponsor an activity in which students act as Web site "critics," debating evaluations of the same Web site and describing their choices for the "best" and "worst" Web sites on a particular topic. You might want to videotape some of these debates to show to parents at a PTO meeting or Parents' Night.

Our next gem comes from Pamela Revercomb, library media specialist at Chittenango (New York) High School. Pamela planned and co-taught this lesson with her intern, Wendy Scalfaro, a graduate student in the Master of Library Science program at Syracuse University and Lynne Pascale, a Participation in Government teacher. They decided to use *WebMAC Senior* with two 12th grade classes (about 50 students) because, "a lot of students think the Internet is the 'source of all information,'" as Pamela stated. "And yet they get so confused and frustrated because they get so many hits," she continued. "Sometimes they'll find an article that sounds right on the topic, but then when they look at it, the teacher or I will point out that this is just Jimmy Joe sitting in his house writing his opinions on things and posting them on the Web. They get upset and embarrassed because it isn't a quality site, and they don't really know what they should have done." Wendy added, "I think kids are drawn in by the novelty of the Web. They're not trained in evaluating whether a site is from a reputable source or somebody just expressing [his] opinion. They not only have to evaluate print resources but [also determine] whether what they're seeing on the Web is reliable." This, they agree, requires new tools like *WebMAC Senior*.

The lesson requires students to come into the library several different times. Their assignment is to choose a controversial social issue and write a five-to-seven page paper that presents both sides of the issue and states their own opinion. Lynne requires them to use four different sources—a book source, one or two Internet sources, a periodical, and a primary document (such as a letter, a diary, or a Supreme Court case). She kicked off the lesson by explaining to students how important it is to evaluate their sources.

The first day Pamela and Wendy introduced a couple of series of books that present opposing viewpoints and explained how students could use them. Then a couple of days later, they showed the students *SIRS Government Reporter*, which contains Supreme Court cases on various subjects. Finally, they introduced students to Electric Library, an online subscription source. The students could choose from a wide range of sources, including magazines and newspapers, books, TV and radio transcripts, photographs, maps, and other items.

The TV and radio transcripts contain congressional testimonies, and the newspapers have editorial letters, which they could use as their primary documents. When Pamela and Wendy introduced Electric Library as a potential source, they thought it was a great opportunity to also teach students how to use *WebMAC Senior*, which Wendy did. The students used it while they did their research that day. "I wanted them to use the instrument while they were doing their research because I thought it would be more relevant," Wendy said.

Because they were concerned that some students might "blow off" the assignment by not visiting the site and instead filling in the instrument any old way, Pamela and Wendy thought of a clever way to monitor that. Since there is no audio at this site, if a student gave a rating for the audio, then they knew that particular evaluation was not reliable. Wendy explained to the students that, for some items, they would be expressing their opinions about the Web site and that there was no right or wrong answer, so they should simply answer how they feel about it. She told them, "One person could feel strongly one way and another feel the opposite, and that [is] okay."

This trio was very happy with the results. Pamela told us, "At this time of year [late spring], these students have 'zero' natural motivation. This got them to focus more on the Web site. We also reminded them that when they went to college and were on their own, they'd need to know how to evaluate the resources they use. That really got their attention." They found the students stayed focused on the tasks and answered all of the questions. Pamela characterized it this way:

> *There was a moment when we were introducing the idea of evaluating Web sites and we actually saw it—the transition from sitting there passively being told what to do, to realizing you're being asked to do critical thinking. The kids realized they were not just going to use the site, they were going to evaluate it. Suddenly, they realized, "Oh, they want our opinion." And "Oh, this is important." Sometimes kids will say, "Am I getting a grade? If not, then I'm not doing it." That didn't happen with this. It was kinda cool watching their faces.*

There were also some unexpected results from this experience. As Pamela told us, "I'm in contact with the webmaster for Electric Library, and he was excited that we had done this. He is really interested in the *WebMAC* results and would like some feedback." It is certainly exciting and a source of satisfaction for both the teachers and the students to know that their evaluations might be used to actually improve a well-known Web site.

Pamela is planning to use the instrument again with the school's other Participation in Government teacher and his classes. She has also been thinking about other ways she might use *WebMAC Senior*, such as when she first shows students how to use the Internet. She thinks this will also help her hone her own Web evaluation skills. She explained, "When I evaluate a Web site for a teacher, for example, so much of [evaluating the quality of the Web sites] happens automatically. So I'd like to review the process periodically with a class in order to keep that fresh in my mind."

NUGGET Arrange to publish a "Web Site of the Month" column in the school newspaper—to which any student may submit an article. Require students to use one of the *WebMAC* instruments to evaluate a Web site of their choice, and then write an article that describes evaluation results and suggest ways the Web site may be used in class assignments.

Our final gem comes from Katherine H. Cronn, library media specialist and Michael Jabot, physics teacher at Oneida (New York) Senior High School. Katherine enjoys working with Michael because he does a lot with his students and the Internet. They collaborated on lessons to teach Michael's 12th grade advanced placement physics students how to evaluate the Web sites they use.

Michael brought his students to the library media center. "We wanted to do this in the library media center rather than the computer lab because we knew the students would take it more seriously," he said. Katherine and Michael introduced the *WebMAC Senior* instrument together, telling the students what they would do and why. Michael wanted them to explore a specific science site, because he wanted their perspective on a comprehensive, multimedia site as "content experts," as well as their feedback on the site's interest and appeal.

Michael describes what they did. "The first day we had them explore the site and use the instrument itself. We followed that up the second day by having them transfer their scores, do the analysis, tally scores, and create a class tally (the site got an "Awesome Web Site" rating)." Katherine then talked with them about what each quadrant of the grid meant.

After the students completed the entire evaluation process, Katherine and Michael decided to let each student choose a site and complete the instrument again. This made it extra motivating because students now had control over what site they would evaluate. They were also familiar with the instrument and felt more confident about completing it. Michael commented, "They were able to fill it out the second time much more quickly and easily. They enjoyed using the instrument and seemed to remember many of the questions because the questions were short, direct, and easy to remember." Katherine agreed, "As Mike said, the questions were short, simple, and something [students] could identify with. There was no question—they understood every item."

When we asked the two educators how the students felt about the experience, Katherine replied, "The kids took it seriously. They were curious about the instrument. We had done some work with them last fall on Web site evaluation, but it came across to the kids as being very 'heavy duty.' [*WebMAC Senior*] didn't look that heavy-duty.

Michael and Katherine are looking forward to using *WebMAC Senior* again next fall with Mike's classes. "I have kids do a lot of independent research, engineering projects," Mike said. "There's such an abundance of information, but unfortunately there's a lot of rotten information also. I think *WebMAC Senior* would be a good evaluation tool for them to use to judge the quality of the sites they find." Katherine added, "I'd also like to use it with the social studies teachers." We hope to revisit Michael and Katherine next year to learn how they used *WebMAC Senior* with a whole new group of students.

NUGGET — **Integrate Web site evaluation into curriculum-related assignments, such as a math lesson on graphing, or have students compare Web evaluations of two or more Web sites on a specific scientific concept.**

COMING UP...

Now that we have shared some real stories from practitioners who described how they used the *WebMAC* instruments to teach students how to evaluate Web sites, we want to show you that there are some other great ways to use the instruments. Read about them in Chapter Nine.

ENDNOTES

[1] K. Schrock, "Evaluation of World Wide Web Sites: An Annotated Bibliography." *ERIC Digest*, June 1998. (EDO-IR-98-02)

HIGHLIGHTS of Chapter Eight

Here are some of the key points covered in Chapter Eight.
▶ Instruments like *WebMAC Senior* provide an exciting opportunity for library media specialists and teachers to work together to plan and teach curriculum-integrated lessons that promote critical evaluation skills.
▶ Teaching critical Web evaluation skills is most effective in the context of authentic projects and assignments.
▶ Many teachers and library media specialists are already using *WebMAC Senior* with their students.

MINESTORMING

Now that you have read Chapter Eight, you probably have a good idea about how some of your colleagues are using *WebMAC Senior* and *WebMAC Middle*. You can adapt some of these ideas (or create new ones) to use with your students. Just use the space below to jot down any great thoughts and ideas you have minestormed from Chapter Eight.

_____

_____

_____

_____

_____

_____

_____

_____

_____

_____

CHAPTER 9

Other Great Ideas for Using *WebMAC Senior*

The Motivation Mining Company

Mine Map

Part I: Motivation Mining for Information Literacy

Part II: Mining Tools for Motivational Assessment

"Other Great Ideas for Using *WebMAC Senior*"

Part IV: Sharing the Wealth

Part III: Panning for Web Gold

Introduction

In Chapter Eight, we shared some stories from teachers and library media specialists who have been using *WebMAC Senior* and *WebMAC Middle* to teach critical evaluation skills to their students. In this chapter, we focus on other ways the instruments have been used with a range of people, including college students and adults. We believe these accounts highlight the versatility of the instruments and may give readers ideas about how to use them in their own situations. For example, we interviewed a library media specialist who is also studying for her master's degree and using the instrument to evaluate Web sites for inclusion in her own "electronic portfolio." One researcher we interviewed translated *WebMAC Senior* into Portuguese and is using the instrument as part of a research project at a university in Brazil. We also spoke with someone who used *WebMAC Senior* to evaluate and improve a newly designed, federally funded Web site on agriculture. As you read this chapter, think about other ways you can envision using the *WebMAC* instruments.

Objectives

When you have finished Chapter Nine, you should:
▶ have an awareness of the variety of uses for *WebMAC Senior* and *WebMAC Middle*.
▶ feel inspired to think of and try new ideas of your own!

More Gems and Nuggets from the "MasterMines"

As we mentioned in Chapter Three, there are other uses for the *WebMAC Senior* and *WebMAC Middle* instruments, beyond using them as tools for teaching students critical evaluation skills. For example, the instruments can be used as lesson-planning tools that help educators select Web sites to include in their lessons or assignments. They also can be used as a research and design tool to collect data about a particular Web site, or as guidelines for what features to include in a new Web site. Here are some more gems and nuggets that describe these alternative ways to use the instruments.

WebMAC Senior for Lesson-Planning

In Chapter Eight, we focused on ways educators used *WebMAC Senior* to teach student evaluation skills; the students, themselves, were the evaluators. *WebMAC Senior* may also be used by educators as their own personal evaluation tool when making decisions about which Web sites are most appropriate for use in their instruction.

Our first lesson-planning gem comes from a library media specialist who used *WebMAC Middle* to help her select the Web sites she will recommend to the teachers in her school.

Gail Gilland is the library media specialist at Damascus (Virginia) Middle School, and she is also pursuing her master's degree in instructional technology at Virginia Polytechnical Institute. The program she is taking at Virginia Tech will culminate with her developing a personal "electronic portfolio" on the Web. We asked Gail what her portfolio would contain. "It will have my resume. It will have educational links that I am recommending, which can be in any categories that I come up with. My professional presentations that I do throughout the course will be posted on the Web all under the umbrella of this portfolio. I will even include software evaluations," she explained.

As Gail mentioned, part of her portfolio will include educational links that she basically is endorsing. As a professional, visitors to her Web page would expect expert recommendations. That puts pressure on Gail to use her personal judgment about which Web sites would be most appropriate or valuable to her colleagues. This makes evaluation especially important to her. "Every time I get on the Web now whether I am here at school or at home doing homework for my portfolio, I am constantly in the 'evaluate' mode," she said. So Gail uses the instrument as a checklist to make decisions about which sites to include as links in her portfolio.

Gail also finds the instrument useful for helping her in a presentation course she is taking at Virginia Tech. "Right now, we are doing presentations every two to three days—electronic presentations on different things—so I'm having to go to a lot of Web sites to pick up information. Time is of the essence... and I find this instrument allows me to quickly go through the site."

Here's another gem of an idea. This one illustrates how *WebMAC Senior* can be used with faculty at the college level.

One of Tim Domick's job responsibilities in his position at Syracuse University's Faculty Academic Computing Support Services (FACSS) is to teach Web development workshops for faculty. Faculty members from throughout the campus attend these workshops. Typically, they are seasoned educators who have been using presentation software in their courses and now want to take another technology leap—to the Web. "One of the challenges I have recently been addressing in these workshops, besides design, has been evaluation," Tim told us. "There is a strong desire from the faculty participants of these seminars to 'know' more about what their students think of the Web sites they have developed and are integrating into their instruction."

So Tim and his colleagues at FACSS are revising their Web development workshops to include an evaluation component. "We have found that *WebMAC*... is exactly the type of tool to be incorporated into this instructional component," he said. They will modify *WebMAC Senior* to "better reflect the needs of our faculty" and use it in upcoming Web development workshops. Tim hopes that some of the professors who attend the workshops will then use it with their students. "I hope they'll use *WebMAC Senior* as a model so that faculty who decide to use it have a place to start," Tim concluded. We think this is a great way to introduce faculty (and eventually their students) to the importance of Web site evaluation for teaching and learning.

Our last gem that demonstrates how to use *WebMAC* as a lesson-planning tool comes from a district media coordinator who has introduced the *WebMAC* instruments to the media specialists in her class and will soon share them with the media specialists in her school district.

Linda Stelter, media coordinator for the Eau Claire (Wisconsin) Area School District, is using the *WebMAC* instruments with the students in a graduate-level course entitled "Media Specialists Community of Learners" that she teaches as an extension course of the University of Wisconsin–Eau Claire (UWEC).

Awareness and understanding of educational standards is an important topic for this audience, so Linda's class focuses on Wisconsin's Model Academic Standards for Information and Technology Literacy. These standards emphasize teaching students to evaluate information resources as early as grade 4 (as we discovered in Chapter Eight, library media specialists are introducing these important skills even earlier than that!). Here's what Linda told us in her own words.

> *The Research Process of our Information Skills Curriculum includes evaluation of information sources as an important step. This year, when our Wide Area Network became available, students began to use Web sites as sources for information.*

> *During the UWEC class, the media specialists looked at various ways for students and teachers to evaluate Web sites. What they found outstanding about the WebMAC instruments was the evaluation of the motivational quality and functional aspects of the Web sites. Also, the three levels of WebMACs*

really make it a versatile tool to use with students of all levels.

This year, we will be undertaking curriculum revision and standards alignment activities. I'm hoping to introduce WebMACs to teachers and students to use as a standard tool. Thank you very much for making this fine resource available.

WebMAC Senior for Research and Design

WebMAC Senior is also a beneficial tool to use when conducting research projects to analyze user responses and perceptions about a Web site in order to make recommendations for modification or revision. It also serves as a useful checklist when designing an original site. Our first gem comes from a pair of statistics instructors at a Midwestern university who were looking for a way to evaluate and improve their course Web sites.

Christopher Bilder and Chris Malone (we'll refer to them as Chris B. and Chris M.), both statistics instructors at Kansas State University, Manhattan, KS, had been looking for a way to assess the usefulness of their course Web sites. They discovered *WebMAC* through their literature review for a paper they are currently writing.

Chris B. teaches an introductory business statistics class. Most of the students are business majors, and this class is the second introductory statistics class that they are required to take. Chris B. gave a slightly modified form of *WebMAC Senior* to his students. He read the directions with his students and explained that the purpose of the instrument was to evaluate the course Web site. Students who completed the instrument would be given five points toward their final grade.

Being a statistician, Chris B. took all of the completed instruments and entered the data into a spreadsheet. From there he graphed and plotted the data in order to view the data in various ways. He even turned the scoring grid into a scatter plot so he could see how the intersection points for all of his students clustered.

Chris B. said he found out that his Web site, in general, was "highly motivating." He added, "[But] there are enough students whose scores fall in the 'needs some improvement' category for [some of the attribute] areas that suggest that I maybe should consider ways to improve these areas." He also conducted an item analysis to identify specific areas that may need improvement, demonstrating the level of detail of feedback information available with this instrument. For example, he found that the students gave a fairly low rating to an item about a "help" function to which he responded, "I am not sure if I will add a 'help function' to my Web site, but I will consider adding more helpful features on [how to use] the Web site." This illustrates that the choice of whether the Web site should be revised and the type of revision to make is completely in the hands of the site designer. Chris B. intends to make some revisions and then use *WebMAC Senior* with his students again the next time he teaches this course.

Chris M. decided that he, too, would like to use *WebMAC Senior* to assess his undergraduate statistics course Web site. He thinks Web evaluation is important because, in his words, "the amount of time someone spends at a site is directly related to how your site looks, how user-friendly it is, and the perceptions people have about your site." Although he felt pretty confident about the content at his site, he wasn't as certain about how well he was capturing and maintaining the interest of his students. As he explained, "I wanted them to continue to be interested in statistics" as a result of using his Web site.

Chris M. administered *WebMAC Senior* with the 85 undergraduate students in his two second-semester statistics classes. He gave the instrument to his students as an extra credit assignment. He wanted them to be critical, so he told them to be thorough and take their time filling it out.

After the students returned their completed instruments, Chris M. entered the data into a spreadsheet and analyzed the results. When he plotted the scores on the scoring grid, he found that his site wasn't quite an Awesome Web Site yet, but he was close. "I was quite pleased with it," he remarked. "It was a nice way to evaluate the efficiency of my Web site and that's what I was after."

Based on the results of this evaluation, Chris M. is planning to make some adjustments to his Web site and then use *WebMAC Senior* again next semester as a homework or extra credit assignment. We bet that next time his site will move up into the Awesome Web Site rating!

The two instructors plan to compare results. Chris M. said, "Since we teach the same class, this comparison may help me [determine] areas in which he may be doing a better job than I. Through examining how [Chris B's] Web site presents these areas, I hope to improve my Web site." We think the comparison will be of mutual benefit to both instructors.

In the next two gems, *WebMAC Senior* was used to evaluate Web sites as part of federally funded research projects.

One of the goals of the Food and Fiber Systems Literacy Project (FFSLP) at Oklahoma State University, Stillwater, OK, funded by a W.K. Kellogg Foundation research grant, was to create an electronic clearinghouse and database support system for developing agricultural knowledge in youths. The Food and Fiber Systems Literacy Web site was originally developed primarily for use by its Project educators, but it later became accessible to the general public. Dan Hubert, Ph.D., a senior research associate on the project (and currently assistant professor at The Southwest Center for Agricultural Health, Injury Prevention and Education) describes how *WebMAC Senior* became an important part of this project. "An assessment of users' perceptions regarding Web site characteristics and overall usability was necessary to affirm [our Web site's] educational merit," Dan stated. "Therefore, to provide the most useful Web site for educators, a need existed to ascertain the quality and functionality of the FFSLP Web site as perceived by educators."

As a result, Dan and his colleagues at Oklahoma State University used an early version of *WebMAC Senior* to collect perceptions about the motivational quality of their Web site from both project and nonproject participants. Results found both groups' scores for the FFSLP Web site were nearly equal. "Based on the *WebMAC* rating scale, the Food and Fiber Systems Literacy Web site was somewhat motivating, but there was room for improvement," Dan said. The results provided important feedback for improvement of the site. They also plan to conduct further research using the *WebMAC* instrument with Web sites of similar content for comparative purposes.

Another research project involving the evaluation of a federal government Web site is our next gem.

A study team for the Department of Education Web site evaluation project at Syracuse University used *WebMAC Senior* to gather and analyze data about users' experiences with the Department of Education site[1]. The team asked two groups of adult users—a group of "expert" Web searchers and a group of "novice" Web searchers—to evaluate the site using the *WebMAC* assessment tool. "The *WebMAC* tool provided a convenient and easy way to gather data about these two groups' experiences," reported Kristin Eschenfelder, a senior research assistant on the project. "Using the *WebMAC* analysis protocols, it was easy to analyze the differences in how the two groups assessed the site."

WebMAC's easy-to-use scoring grids permit researchers to gain a quick understanding of the differences between sites and between users' perceptions. In this case, the study team wanted to identify any differences between experts' and novices' reactions to the Department of Education Web site. This information then allowed the researchers to suggest modifications in the site to meet the needs of these two important user groups.

A team of researchers from Brazil also found *WebMAC Senior* invaluable in assessing their Web-based course for teachers.

Anise Ferreira, Ph.D., and Heloisa Collins, Ph.D., researchers of EDULANG, a project of the Graduate Program in Applied Linguistics at the Catholic University of Sao Paulo, Brazil, are exploring online language learning, course and material design and evaluation, and the effects of interface on learning. The investigation is being conducted within the perspective of modern applied linguistics.

The team has been working on the development of Web-based courses, which are being used as sources of data for the research group. The target population of these courses has included teachers of English in Brazilian state high schools and adult learners of English as Foreign Language. Course aims have focused on reading, writing, and oral comprehension. Anise translated *WebMAC Senior* (and is in the process of translating *WebMAC Junior*) into Portuguese. She hopes to use the latter tool in the future with elementary school teachers.

Anise used *WebMAC Senior* to evaluate the motivational aspects of the Web-based instruction with about 70 adult Brazilian students enrolled in "Surfing and Learning," an English course for Internet users. *WebMAC* will be also used to evaluate the courses for about 30 schoolteachers of English from several small rural towns. Additionally, *WebMAC* is being used as one data collection instrument for the EDULANG research group. "*WebMAC* will give us a very important picture of part of this complex thing called learning on the Internet," Heloisa predicted.

Our next gem finds *WebMAC Senior* being used to help identify the reasons why a specific group of targeted users *aren't* visiting a Web site.

Elena Lopez Mateos, a graduate student in the Department of Educational Technology at San Diego State University, is using *WebMAC Senior* to conduct a formative evaluation of the Latin American Consortium Web page for the Getty Conservation Institute (GCI). Elena explained, "The GCI is considered the main authority in preventive conservation and has formed a consortium of five Latin American countries. The Consortium is being viewed as a possible model for an 'electronic teaching community' for other regions of the world [such as eastern Europe and Russia], so it would be very useful to learn as much as possible from this first attempt."

The Consortium is trying to build a network of about 1,500 specialists (e.g., chemists, architects, curators) in preventive conservation that will allow participants to create and share their knowledge and resources. "The GCI has taken on the responsibility of providing a way for the consortium members to benefit from their collective knowledge; that is why the Consortium Web Page was created," Elena said.

"The Web page has been up and running from the beginning of this year, and so far the consortium members are not taking advantage of the information hosted on the site; in other words they are not using the Web page," she continued. Therefore, Elena intends to use *WebMAC Senior* to determine the answer to her question: How well does the Web site meet the needs and goals of the Consortium members? There are actually two issues to consider here—Are Consortium members not returning after having visited the Web site? Or have they *never* visited the Web site, and, thus, there is a promotional issue. (It will be interesting to find out, after Elena completes her research, where the problem actually lies.) Once she finds out what is wrong, she can make recommendations for improvement.

There are plans to use *WebMAC Senior* to evaluate an important science Web site. We describe this situation in our next gem.

John Chadwick, Ed.D., is Senior Research Associate at the Institute for Learning Innovation (ILI), a private nonprofit organization in Annapolis, Maryland, that conducts research and evaluation in free-choice learning environments. The Institute and the New York Hall of Science are seeking funding for research on how the public uses science education Web sites. They want to know who uses these sites and for what purposes. John plans to use *WebMAC Senior* and *WebMAC Middle* as two of their data collection tools. John told us, "The *WebMAC* instruments will be invaluable for allowing us to assess whether the Web site even holds the attention of the online learner."

One of the authors used *WebMAC Senior* in her course entitled "Motivational Aspects of Information Use." Students were divided into three research teams. Each team selected one of three small business Web sites to evaluate and conducted the evaluation using *WebMAC Senior*. Each team compiled its results and wrote an evaluation report citing the site's strengths, providing suggestions for improvement, and submitting it to the business' webmaster. All three businesses used the suggestions to improve their sites, and the students used the experience to make connections between motivation, evaluation, and Web resources.

The *WebMAC Senior* items can also be used as guidelines for the design of new Web sites. In this way, the instrument truly serves as a checklist for designers.

Remember earlier in this chapter when we described how Gail Gilland used *WebMAC Middle* as a way of evaluating the Web sites that she may include as links in her electronic portfolio? Well, Gail also is using *WebMAC Middle* for designing and modifying the school Web site at Damascus Middle School where she is the webmaster. Gail is able to use *WebMAC Middle* from an adult perspective while constantly trying to maintain the eyes of a child, something her years of experience gives her the ability to do. She thinks *WebMAC Middle* is especially well-suited for middle school aged children. She explained, " I found [the items] very clear and concise. I think some of the other models [were] meant for adults' eyes only, and yet they were saying 'this is an activity that you can do with your students.' And I didn't feel like it was. In fact, it was way too over their heads." An important feature of the *WebMAC* instruments is that they were designed for and tested by kids.

When Gail first started designing the Web site two years ago, she said she to put "all these little animations and doodads in all over the place." However, that soon changed. "Once I started reviewing evaluation instruments like yours, knowing what makes a good Web page and what doesn't, and really defining what you want your page to be, it's different..." she said.

Now Gail asks herself questions like "Do I want this page to be strictly a showcase for my school with lots of pictures of kids and things that will take forever to download, or do I want it to be more of a jumping off point for my teachers and students so they can use their school's Web page as their own home page?" She wants *teachers* to be able to go to the school's page and be able to access sites that can be immediately helpful to them in the classroom. She also wants *students* to be able to access their school page from home and know that she, personally, has put some sites on the page that they can use for reports. Gail said, "I want to be very picky about the pages that I put on their [school Web site]." Gail said she wants the pages to be authoritative, designed well but not "take forever to download," and to be of help to students and teachers.

The authors are using *WebMAC Senior* as a guideline for the ongoing design of their motivation-related Web site (www.MotivationMining.com).

NUGGET

COMING UP...

In Chapter Ten, we offer some final thoughts on the importance of evaluation skills for the information literate citizen of the 21st century.

ENDNOTES

[1] C. A. Hert, K. R. Eschenfelder, C. R. McClure, J. Rubin, M. D. Taffet, J. E. Abend, and D. M. Pimentel, *Evaluation of Selected Websites at the U.S. Department of Education: Increasing Access to Web-Based Resources.* Syracuse, NY: Information Institute of Syracuse, January 1999. <http://iis.syr.edu/webeval/>.

HIGHLIGHTS of Chapter Nine

Here are some of the key points covered in Chapter Nine.
The *WebMAC* instruments have many uses:

▶ They can be used for planning lessons, helping in the decision-making process that determines which Web sites to use in classroom presentations and homework assignments.

▶ They can be used in research to evaluate and compare existing Web sites.

▶ They can be used as design tools for guiding the creation of effective new Web sites.

MINESTORMING

After reading Chapter Nine, you probably have some ideas about some other ways to use *WebMAC Senior* (and *WebMAC Middle*) that no one else has thought of. Make sure to record them below.

_____
_____
_____
_____
_____
_____
_____
_____
_____
_____

Chapter 10

Motivation Mining into the Future

Introduction

All one needs to do is pay close attention to recent commercials on television to realize how much technology has changed our world. Ads for technology applications, hardware, software, and electronic services flood the airwaves. And almost every ad ends with a Web site address—just one more indication that the children of the next millenium must not only be comfortable with using technology but must also be wise consumers of technology. This requires new skills and new tools.

Objectives

By the end of this chapter, you will be able to:
▶ understand the need for Web evaluation skills for the information literate citizen of the 21st century.
▶ synthesize the main concepts described in this book

Information Skills for the 21st Century

Today's students are on the crest of a technology wave that is sweeping not only the country, but also the world. The information literate citizen of the 21st century must possess the skills needed to effectively use technology and to add value to its potential applications. In his book *The Road Ahead*, Bill Gates looks back at the difficulty we once had in locating the best information for our needs and recalls the amount of time it took to find that information. He contrasts that with today's electronic search capabilities and our ability to access information in different ways than we ever did before. "[This] flexibility invites exploration, and the exploration is invariably rewarded with discovery."[1]

But discovery is not enough—it is only part of the exploration process. In the 19th century, California Gold Rush miners used maps and word-of-mouth to search for gold, but it was their ability to "sift" and "differentiate" between real gold and its imposters that led them to the limited riches available. As we enter the 21st century, the Web continues to grow at an explosive rate, and the riches available to everyone are almost limitless. As new technologies emerge and evolve, the speed and quality of all forms of information and the level of interactivity available—what Bill Gates calls "the global interactive network"—provides access even to those in the most isolated parts of the world. The sheer amount of information on the Web makes using all of it impossible; the differences in quality among Web resources make using all of it undesirable. The ability to evaluate and identify the highest quality Web resources is becoming critical.

We have only just begun to uncover the treasures that lay beneath the surface of the Web and to refine the beneficial resources available for the taking. Successful information miners will possess the skills and tools to find the solutions to tomorrow's problems, rather than spin their wheels still trying to figure out the questions.

Learning critical evaluation skills within a total information literacy program is essential for today's students to "thrive in an information rich future."[2] As educators, we must be sure that these skills and tools are within the grasp of all of our students to empower them to "stake their claim" and compete in the 21st century.

Final Thoughts

Throughout this book, we used a mining metaphor to provide a framework for evaluating the rich resources of the World Wide Web. We began by describing the importance of and relationships among information literacy, motivation, and the evaluation of Web resources. We then introduced some innovative Web evaluation instruments that focus on the motivational quality of Web sites while considering their content and functional capabilities. These "mining tools" were designed for students but may also be used by teachers, library media specialists, and others concerned with identifying the best resources for teaching and learning. We followed this with descriptions of a variety of practical applications for these tools, most of which came from K-12 educators, college instructors, and researchers.

We hope that the readers of this book will come away with a bonanza of ideas that they can implement to meet their needs and the needs of their students. We invite readers to submit their Web evaluation success stories to us at our Web site (www.MotivationMining.com) so that they may be shared with the larger education community.

COMING UP...

In Chapter Eleven, we provide all of the materials needed for an inservice workshop on Web evaluation for educators.

ENDNOTES

[1] B. Gates, *The Road Ahead.* Penguin Books, (Rev. ed.), 1996, pp. 135-6.

[2] M. B. Eisenberg and D. Johnson. "Computer Skills for Information Problem-Solving: Learning and Teaching Technology in Context." *ERIC Digest.* Clearinghouse on Information & Technology, March 1996, p.4. (EDO-IR-96-04)

HIGHLIGHTS of Chapter Ten

Here are some of the key points covered in Chapter Ten.

▶ In order to be productive and contributing citizens of the 21st century, today's students must not only learn the skills necessary to be truly information literate, but they must also be capable of adding value to present technology applications. Furthermore, they must be thinking of new and creative ways to use the vast amount of information that is available to them.

▶ Educators and students must possess essential evaluation skills and use effective evaluation tools to identify the highest quality Web resources for teaching and learning.

MINESTORMING

Although Chapter Ten was brief, it may have stirred some thoughts that you will want to preserve. Use this page to jot them down.

_____
_____
_____
_____
_____
_____
_____
_____
_____
_____

PART IV

Sharing the Wealth

CHAPTER 11

A Workshop for Educators

The Motivation Mining Company

Mine Map

Part I: Motivation Mining for Information Literacy

Part II: Mining Tools for Motivational Assessment

"A Workshop for Educators"

Part IV: Sharing the Wealth

Part III: Panning for Web Gold

Introduction

Now that you have learned several ways to use *WebMAC Senior* with your students, you may want to share your knowledge with some of your colleagues. In this chapter, we provide everything you need (a lesson content outline, reproducible overhead transparency and handout masters, and a certificate of achievement) to conduct a professional workshop for educators on using *WebMAC Senior* (and *WebMAC Middle*).

Objectives

After completing this chapter, you will be able to:
▶ provide a workshop for educators on Evaluating Web Resources.
▶ demonstrate how to use *WebMAC Senior* with your students.

Materials:

Participants will need:
▶ A computer lab or enough computers for participants to work individually or in pairs.
▶ Copies of *WebMAC Senior*, directions, and scoring grids.

Workshop Outline

The following outline (or script) is intended to be a guide for your presentation. Feel free to embellish, modify, or add your own touches to the content. Each number corresponds to the related slide.

1. This workshop is entitled "Motivating Mining the Web: Inservice Workshop for Secondary Educators." As workshop facilitator, you must **capture the interest and attention** of your workshop participants. One way of introducing the workshop is to cite the hottest statistics you can find on Internet usage, the soaring number of Web sites, and the high degree of student dependency on the World Wide Web as a source of their research for school assignments. This will help set the stage for the need for students to develop critical evaluation skills in order to identify and evaluate the highest quality Web sites available.
You might want to begin by asking questions of the audience to get them in a participatory mood (e.g., "Does anyone know how often information doubles?"). Make sure you have the *latest* statistics. After warming up your

audience, use your overheads to reinforce the main points using this content outline as a basic guide.

2. Review the workshop's leaning objectives. Stress the point that participants will leave with ideas for teaching students how to evaluate Web resources.
3. You will want to define the term *Motivation Mining*—the identification and extraction of Web resources that have the potential of engaging students in the learning process by meeting important motivational criteria. This requires "sifting" through many Web sites to find the "gems."
4. The principles of Motivation Mining and the Web evaluation instrument are based on a well-known motivation theory, Expectancy-Value (or E-V) Theory. E-V theory states that there are two prerequisites for a person to be motivated to complete a task.
5. Tell participants that the first prerequisite of E-V Theory is that the person must value the task. The second prerequisite is that the person must *expect to succeed* at the task.
6. Explain that there are two critical factors to consider when evaluating Web resources for teaching and learning. The first factor is CONTENT VALIDITY. When considering content, we must decide whether it is *appropriate* for the specific teaching need (e.g., on the appropriate learning level, curriculum-related,) and whether the source of the site is authentic; that is credible and authoritative for this topic. But content validity is not enough when evaluating Web resources.
7. Continue by saying that the second critical factor is MOTIVATIONAL QUALITY; that is, the potential of the selected Web site to motivate students to learn. If a Web site is high in Motivational Quality, students will want to remain at the Web site and explore it and will revisit it for future learning.
8. Remind participants that like E-V Theory, Motivational Quality also has two factors: Value and Expectation for Success. For Web sites, Value means providing information and activities that students perceive as valuable and personally relevant. Expectation for Success means providing an environment in which students feel confident that they can be successful in navigating and using the Web site. At this point, you might want to ask your workshop participants to brainstorm some Web features that might foster value and an expectation for success in students.
9. Emphasize that the two factors of Motivational Quality are also multiplicative. Both must be present for the Web site to be successfully motivating.
10. Tell participants that Motivational Quality is defined in terms of four attributes.
11. Two attributes, Stimulating and Meaningful, relate to Value; while Organized and Easy to Use describe Expectation for Success.
12. Explain that for a Web site to be Stimulating, it must contain features that

capture and maintain interest and stimulate curiosity. A Meaningful Web site has elements that add personal value and promote relevance. (Try brainstorming ideas for adding value, if you have time.)

13. An Organized Web site has features that provide a logical overall structure and sequence to facilitate understanding of the Web site's content. A Web site is *Easy to Use* when it includes various navigation aids and help mechanisms.

14. Ask participants what makes the Web evaluation instrument different than others you might know? Three ways: (1) it has a theoretical base (E-V Theory), (2) it focuses on *motivational* issues and (3) it was designed for use by students. Although it focuses on motivational issues, it covers many issues that should be considered when evaluating Web sites in general. Thus, it is widely used as a general evaluation instrument.

15. Mention that the *Website Motivational Analysis Checklist* (*WebMAC*, for short) is available at three levels: *WebMAC Junior* for grades 1-4; *WebMAC Middle* for grades 5-8; and *WebMAC Senior* for grade 9 and up. All are based on E-V Theory. Today, we will focus on *WebMAC Senior*. These instruments have been widely tested and validated. As they will soon see, the *WebMACs* provide a set of grids for visually representing scores.

16. Tell participants that *WebMAC Senior* can be used in three ways. It can be used to teach students important evaluation skills as part of an information literacy program. It can be used as a lesson-planning tool for identifying the best Web resources to incorporate into lessons or students' homework assignments. It can also be used as a research and design tool to compare Web sites or provide guidance for design of a new Web site.

17. [Select a Web site that participants can evaluate during the workshop. Pass out copies of the instrument and go through directions. Give them sufficient time to complete the instrument (approximately 45 minutes). When they have finished, have them reconvene and review the scoring mechanisms with them. Debrief on results.]

18. [Have participants brainstorm ways they could use *WebMAC Senior* with their students in their subject areas.] Mention that for the upper elementary grades, the *WebMAC Middle* instrument might be useful because of its simpler language and fewer items. Both instruments have the same theoretical framework. Scoring differences are explained in the administration directions. (It is your decision whether to provide the *WebMAC Middle* instrument as part of your workshop.)

Overhead Transparency Masters

On the next 18 pages you will find a set of reproducible overhead transparency masters which you may use in a workshop on *WebMAC Senior* (and *WebMAC Middle*) for your colleagues.

Motivation Mining the Web

Inservice Workshop for Secondary Educators

Motivation Mining the Web

Workshop participants will:

▼ understand the concept and principles of "motivation mining" for educators.

▼ recognize the critical factors in evaluating Web sites.

▼ understand the role of *Value* and *Expectation for Success* and their attributes in assessing motivational quality.

▼ be able to teach their students about Web site evaluation using *WebMAC Senior*.

What is Motivation Mining?

"Motivation Mining"

for educators is the identification and extraction of Web resources that have the potential of engaging students in the learning process by meeting important motivational criteria.

As in mining in the traditional sense, one must "sift" through many Web sites in search of the "gems."

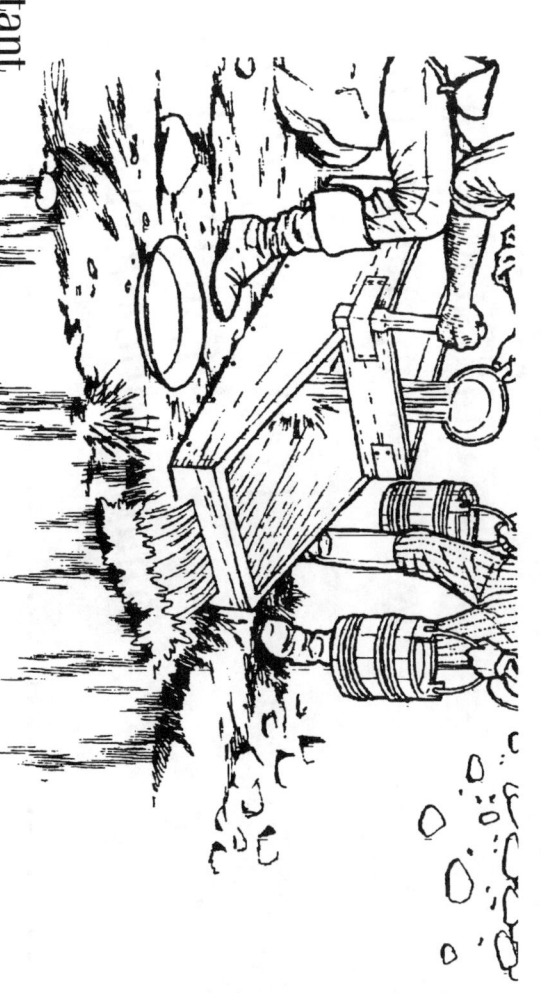

Theory

The principles of Motivation Mining are grounded primarily in Expectancy-Value Theory (E-V)

E-V Theory states that there are two prerequisites for a person to be motivated to complete a task.

E-V Theory

The person must VALUE the task.

The person must have an EXPECTATION FOR SUCCESS at the task.

Critical Factors in Evaluating Web Sites...

Teacher judgments of content validity

Appropriateness

Authenticity

YOU are the judge!

This factor is a NECESSARY but INSUFFICIENT condition.

Critical Factors in Evaluating Web Sites...

Student Perceptions of Motivational Quality

Determines the potential of the selected Web site to motivate students to learn.

If the motivational quality is high, students:

▼ will want to remain at Web site and explore.

▼ may wish to revisit the Web site at another time for future learning experiences.

Motivational Quality of Web Sites

Value

The Web site provides information and activities that students perceive as *stimulating* and *meaningful*.

Expectation for Success

The Web site should provide an *organized* and *easy-to-use* environment in which students feel confident that they can be successful in navigating and using the Web site.

Motivational Quality of Web Sites

Multiplicative Function:

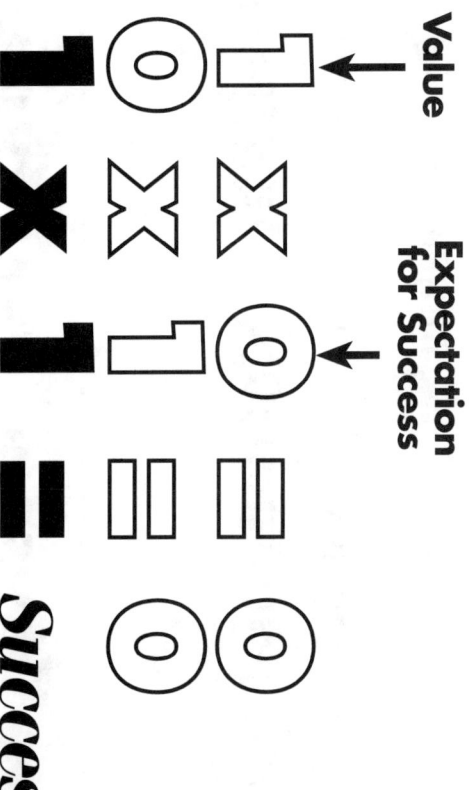

Value ↓
1   0   1
x   x   x
0 ← 1   1
=   =   =
0   0   **Success!**

Expectation for Success

The number "1" refers to the presence of a factor, while "0" refers to the absence of a factor.

Critical Factors in Evaluating Web Sites...

A Web Site's Motivational Quality

The degree to which a Web site is:

- ▼ stimulating
- ▼ meaningful
- ▼ organized
- ▼ easy-to-use

Attributes Affecting E and V

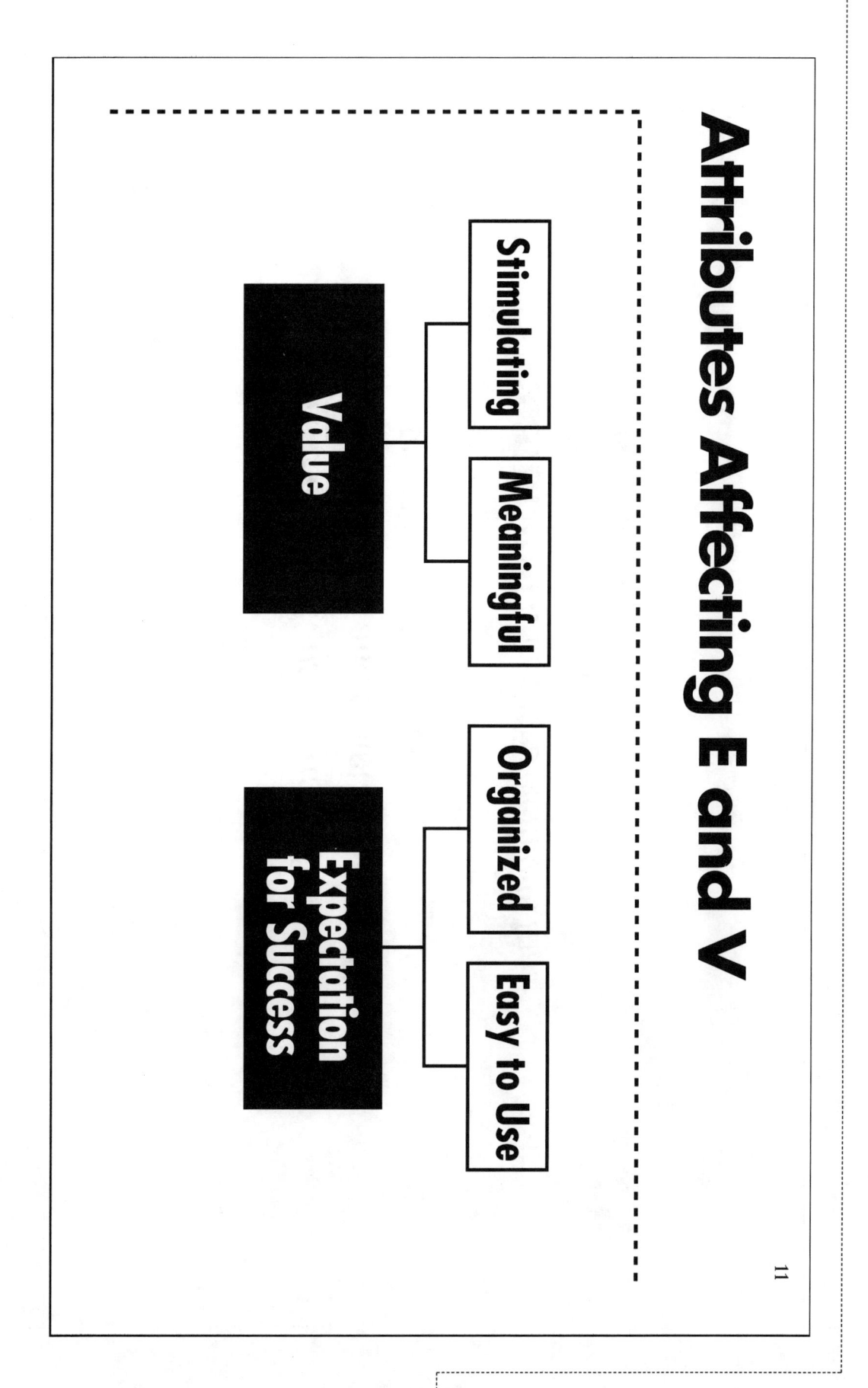

- **Value**
  - Stimulating
  - Meaningful

- **Expectation for Success**
  - Organized
  - Easy to Use

Value

Stimulating: *has features that*
- ▼ capture and maintain interest
- ▼ stimulate curiosity

Meaningful: *includes elements that*
- ▼ add personal value
- ▼ promote relevance

Expectation for Success

Organized: *has features that*
- ▼ provide a logical overall structure
- ▼ facilitate understanding of the Web site's content

Easy-to-use: *includes elements such as*
- ▼ navigational aids
- ▼ help mechanisms

Motivational Assessment

- There are many Web evaluation tools.
- Few have a theoretical base.
- Most focus on content or functionality (how well the navigational mechanisms work).
- Few address motivational issues.

Motivational Assessment

Web Site Motivational Analysis Checklist (WebMAC)©

▼ set of three instruments for use of students
  ▽ *WebMAC Junior–2000* for grades 1-4
  ▽ *WebMAC Middle* for grades 5-8
  ▽ *WebMAC Senior* for grades 9 and up
▼ based on E-V theory
▼ tested and validated
▼ provides set of grids for visually representing scores

Motivational Assessment

WebMAC Senior can be used:

▼ to help teach students evaluation skills, an important aspect of information literacy.

▼ as a lesson-planning tool when you are evaluating a Web site for use in any curricular unit.

▼ as a research and design tool for practitioners conducting their own research on motivational effectiveness of Web sites or designing a new Web site.

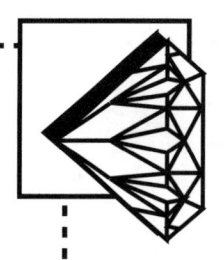

Using WebMAC Senior to Mine Web "Gems"

▼ The Directions
▽ Administration
▽ Scoring
▼ The WebMAC Senior instrument
▼ Practice
▼ Debrief

"MINE" STORMING

Let's think of some ideas for using ***WebMAC Senior*** with students.

Handouts

On the next four pages you will find reproducible handouts and a certificate of achievement for the participants in your workshop for educators.

Motivation Mining the Web

Inservice Workshop for Secondary Educators

Motivation Mining the Web

Workshop participants will:
- ▶ understand the concept and principles of "motivation mining" for educators.
- ▶ recognize the critical factors in evaluating Web sites.
- ▶ understand the role of *Value* and *Expectation for Success* and their attributes in assessing motivational quality.
- ▶ be able to teach their students about Web site evaluation using *WebMAC Senior*.

What is Motivation Mining?

"Motivation Mining" for educators is the identification and extraction of Web resources that have the potential of engaging students in the learning process by meeting important motivational criteria.

As in mining in the traditional sense, one must "sift" through many Web sites in search of the "gems."

Theory

The principles of *Motivation Mining* are grounded primarily in Expectancy-Value Theory (E-V)

E-V Theory states that there are two prerequisites for a person to be motivated to complete a task.

E-V Theory

The person must VALUE the task.

The person must have an EXPECTATION FOR SUCCESS at the task.

Critical Factors in Evaluating Web Sites...

Teacher judgments of content validity

Appropriateness

Authenticity

YOU are the judge!

This factor is a NECESSARY but INSUFFICIENT condition.

Slide 7: Critical Factors in Evaluating Web Sites...

Student Perceptions of Motivational Quality

Determines the potential of the selected Web site to motivate students to learn.

If the motivational quality is high, students:
- will want to remain at Web site and explore.
- may wish to revisit the Web site at another time for future learning experiences.

Slide 8: Motivational Quality of Web Sites

Value
The Web site provides information and activities that students perceive as *stimulating* and *meaningful*.

Expectation for Success
The Web site should provide an *organized* and *easy-to-use* environment in which students feel confident that they can be successful in navigating and using the Web site.

Slide 9: Motivational Quality of Web Sites

Multiplicative Function:

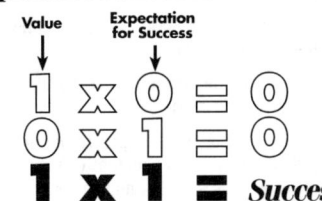

$$1 \text{ (Value)} \times 0 \text{ (Expectation for Success)} = 0$$
$$0 \times 1 = 0$$
$$\mathbf{1 \times 1 =} \textit{Success!}$$

The number "1" refers to the presence of a factor, while "0" refers to the absence of a factor.

Slide 10: Critical Factors in Evaluating Web Sites...

A Web Site's Motivational Quality

The degree to which a Web site is:
- stimulating
- meaningful
- organized
- easy-to-use

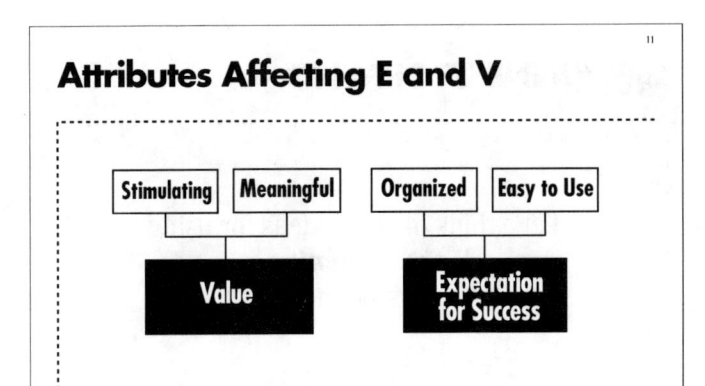

Slide 11: Attributes Affecting E and V

- Stimulating, Meaningful → **Value**
- Organized, Easy to Use → **Expectation for Success**

Slide 12: Value

Stimulating: *has features that*
- capture and maintain interest
- stimulate curiosity

Meaningful: *includes elements that*
- add personal value
- promote relevance

Expectation for Success

Organized: *has features that*
- provide a logical overall structure
- facilitate understanding of the Web site's content

Easy-to-use: *includes elements such as*
- navigational aids
- help mechanisms

Motivational Assessment

There are many Web evaluation tools.

Few have a theoretical base.

Most focus on content or functionality (how well the navigational mechanisms work).

Few address motivational issues.

Motivational Assessment

Web Site Motivational Analysis Checklist (WebMAC)©
- set of three instruments for use of students
  - *WebMAC Junior–2000* for grades 1-4
  - *WebMAC Middle* for grades 5-8
  - *WebMAC Senior* for grades 9 and up
- based on E-V theory
- tested and validated
- provides set of grids for visually representing scores

Motivational Assessment

***WebMAC Senior* can be used:**
- to help teach students evaluation skills, an important aspect of information literacy.
- as a lesson-planning tool when you are evaluating a Web site for use in any curricular unit.
- as a research and design tool for practitioners conducting their own research on motivational effectiveness of Web sites or designing a new Web site.

Using *WebMAC Senior* to Mine Web "Gems"

- The Directions
  - Administration
  - Scoring
- The *WebMAC Senior* instrument
- Practice
- Debrief

"MINE" STORMING

Let's think of some ideas for using
WebMAC Senior
with students.

Certificate of Achievement

Motivation Mining the Web
Inservice Workshop for Secondary Educators

_____
Name

_____
Presented By

_____
Date

COMING UP...

In Chapter Twelve, we present overhead transparency masters and an outline for teaching students about *WebMAC Senior*. These materials are intended to supplement a larger lesson or unit on the evaluation of information resources.

HIGHLIGHTS of Chapter Eleven

Here are some of the key points covered in Chapter Eleven.

▶ You can provide a workshop for your colleagues on motivation mining the Web, using this chapter's workshop outline as a guide.

▶ Overhead transparencies, hand-outs, and a certificate of achievement are included.

▶ Whenever possible, get your audience in a participatory mood by asking questions and getting them involved.

MINESTORMING

Use the workshop outline and materials in this chapter to design your own in-service workshop for teachers, library media specialists, and others who teach students how to evaluate Web sites. Write some of your ideas below.

_____
_____
_____
_____
_____
_____
_____
_____
_____
_____

CHAPTER 12

Teaching Students to Use *WebMAC Senior*

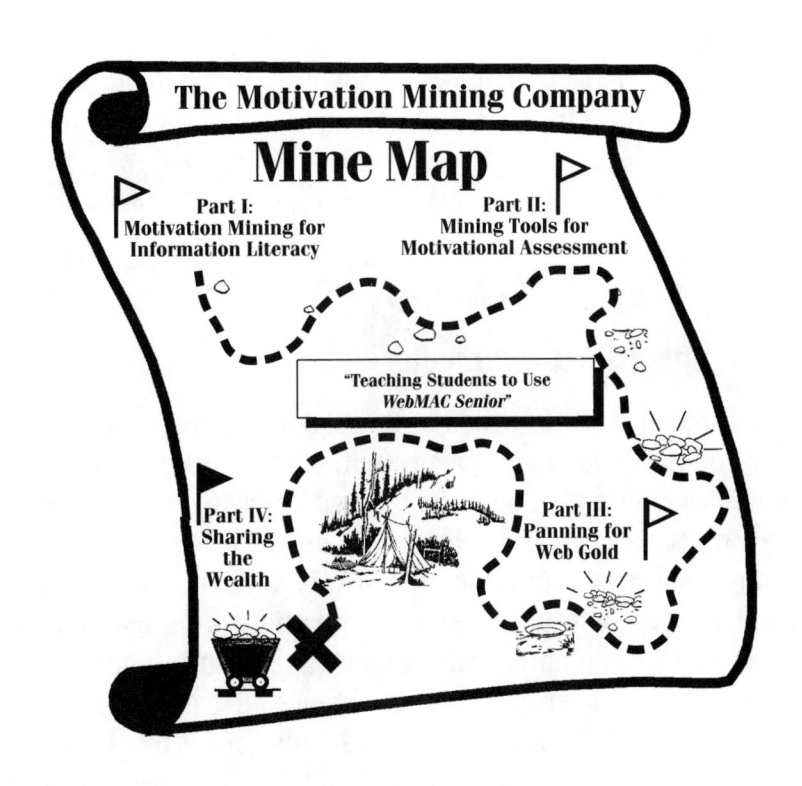

Introduction

Many of the teachers and library media specialists we interviewed mentioned that they were not only designing lessons to teach students about the importance of Web evaluation but were also developing materials to help students learn how to complete the *WebMAC* instruments. Therefore, we decided that the most valuable information we could provide in this final chapter would be overhead transparency masters (with a descriptive outline). You might find them useful, and they will save you time as well. These are not meant to replace your own ideas and creative process but rather to provide additional materials that could be integrated into and enhance whatever lesson or unit you create on evaluation.

Objectives

After completing this chapter, you will be able to:
▶ integrate the overhead masters into your own lesson plan(s).
▶ demonstrate how to use *WebMAC Senior* with your students.

Materials:

You will need:
▶ enough computers so that students may work individually or in pairs; or if working in a group situation, one computer with Internet connection and projection system.
▶ copies of *WebMAC Senior*, directions, scoring sheets, and plotting grids for each student.

Outline for Integrating Overheads

This outline is not intended to be used an independent lesson plan, but it is meant to provide guidance for presenting the overhead transparency slides in this chapter within a lesson that you've designed. Each point in the outline below references the number of the overhead it describes.

1. Introduce the concept of evaluation of Web sites. The overhead title, "We've Got to Look Critically at Web Sites," can initiate a discussion on the reasons why Web resource evaluation is important.
2. Help students to understand the importance of their learning to evaluate Web resources. Reveal and discuss each bullet point one by one to reduce visual overload. The first bullet point can be used to discuss the continuing

explosion of the number of World Wide Web Sites. The second and third bullets can be part of an interactive dialog on what makes a "good" or a "bad" Web site. If students don't mention them, you might want to point out a few important Web features like accuracy, currency, organization, usefulness, and so on. This usually generates many other ideas from students.

3. Have a quick discussion of key terms students should understand before using a Web assessment instrument. These are all terms that will appear on the instrument they will use.

4. Introduce *WebMAC Senior*, handing out copies of the instrument. Stress that it is not a test, and there are no wrong answers. Point out that the instrument measures the motivational quality of a Web site. You might want to review some of the aspects of motivational quality, explaining that the validity of the content and whether the site works the way it should (functionality) also contribute to how motivating (stimulating, meaningful, organized, easy to use) a site is. Students could look for specific items that exemplify these different categories.

5. This overhead outlines the major steps to follow for completing the evaluation. You might want to begin by evaluating (at least in part) a Web site with your students. You can select a Web site and project it on the screen and/or have students locate it on their computers. Ask them to identify the general content of the site and then encourage them to spend some time (15-20 minutes is usually sufficient) exploring the site.

6. Once they have completed this, begin to fill out *WebMAC Senior* together. Go over enough items, until you are sure they understand how the rating system works. If possible, find an item that will be "Not Applicable" to this Web site. This will allow you to explain that some items may refer to features that are not present at the Web site.

7. Describe how after they have completed all items, they will revisit each of their NA items and rate them.

8. Students may then transfer their item scores into the four scoring columns and add up their column scores. Briefly review the meaning of each motivational quality category.

9. The students can plot their four scores on the graph. Ask them how it helps to share their graphs with you and each other. You could ask them to explain what the graph means about this Web site. It might also be fun to discuss differences in individual graphs and how scores are dependent on individual judgments and, therefore, will vary. It will be interesting to see if students rate the site similarly, or if there is a wide range of different of scores.

10. Now students can combine their four scores into two main scores: Value and Expectation for Success. This would be a good time to point out how

both of these must be high for a Web site to be considered an "Awesome Web Site."

11. The final items on *WebMAC Senior* require students to answer two questions and then suggest ways to improve the Web site. If you are using *WebMAC Senior* as a group activity, you could solicit responses from your students and write them on the overhead. What some students liked, others may not. This is a good time to reinforce that everyone is expected to have their own opinions when doing an evaluation.

12. You might wish to demonstrate to the group how to plot their individual scores on the overhead and draw the intersection point to show a real example. Or, you could make an example to show (or use ours). Then, review what it means to be in each quadrant (refer to Chapter Seven for interpretation). You might even wish to write this information on the overhead itself as you are explaining, as one teacher we know did. You can reproduce this overhead twice if you also wish to grid the class average scores.

13. Overhead #13 is an overlay to Overhead #12. Once students grasp how to plot their scores, you can add this overlay to demonstrate where outstanding ("Awesome") Web sites fall. You may wish to tape these transparencies together ahead of time so that they align correctly.

14. If you decide to average all the students scores on a particular Web site, you can display this class tally by having each student call out his or her scores for **V** and **XS** as you place them on the overhead. This will keep students' attention, and it is fun for them to compare their scores with others. One LMS told us she used a calculator to quickly tally up and average the scores. Then, she plotted the average scores on the grid for the class to see and discussed the results. With older students, you might want to encourage them to do the math. You could then plot the average scores on the scoring grid (Overhead #12) and again superimpose Overhead #13. Students may want to discuss how their scores differed from the class score and what they learned about evaluating Web sites.

Overhead Transparency Masters

On the following fourteen pages you will find the reproducible overhead transparency masters to be used with the outline above.

Evaluating Information Resources

We've Got to Look Critically at Web Sites!

1

Why Evaluate Web Sites?

- There are huge numbers of Web sites on every imaginable topic.

- How do you know you have found the best Web site(s)?

- How do you know how to improve an existing Web site?

Web Terms

HOME PAGE: the starting place for exploring a Web site. Here you find out what is on the Web site.

HYPERLINK (or LINK): a way of connecting to another source of information.

BUTTON: what you click in order to move from one place to another within the Web site or to activate a particular request.

SITE MAP: similar to a menu, outlines the content and activities included at the site.

NAVIGATION MECHANISMS: used to find various parts of the Web site.

-
-
-
-
-

3

Web Site Evaluation

Website Motivational Analysis Checklist (WebMAC) Senior

- not a test
- no wrong answers
- measures motivational quality

How to Use *WebMAC Senior*

What to do first:

- Identify the general content of the Web site.

- Spend time exploring the Web site to become familiar with its content and structure.

- Rate the Web site using *WebMAC Senior*.

Scoring WebMAC Senior

- Rate each item:

  3 = strongly agree
  2 = somewhat agree
  1 = somewhat disagree
  0 = strongly disagree

  NA = Not Applicable

Scoring WebMAC Senior

- Go back and rate each NA item:

  0 = the Web site would have benefited if it had included the item.
  1 = the Web site didn't require that item.
  2 = the Web site was better off for *not* including that item.

Plotting Your Scores

• Transfer the score for each item in the correct column in the appropriately numbered space.

• Add the numbers in each column and place the total in the bottom space marked "Total."

S = STIMULATING
M = MEANINGFUL
O = ORGANIZED
E = EASY-TO-USE

8

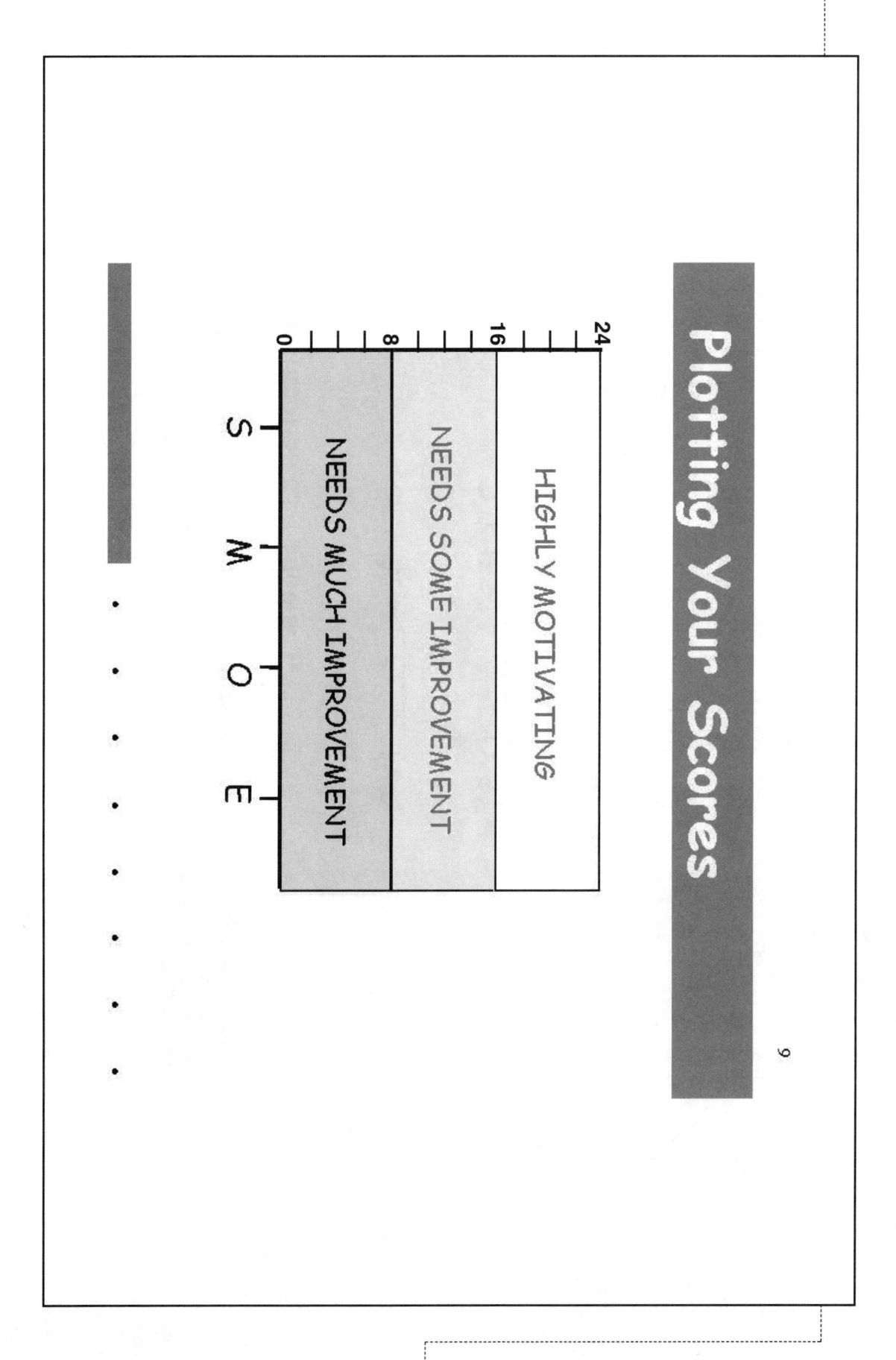

Plotting Your Scores

	S	M	O	E
24				
16	HIGHLY MOTIVATING			
8	NEEDS SOME IMPROVEMENT			
0	NEEDS MUCH IMPROVEMENT			

9

Plotting Your Scores

- Combine scores as follows:

  S + M = _____ (V)

  O + E = _____ (XS)

  V = how VALUABLE this Web site is to you.

  XS = how SUCCESSFUL you expect to be at this Web site.

General Items

I would visit this Web site again.   YES/NO

I would recommend this Web site to others.   YES/NO

What is the best thing about this Web site?

What needs improvement at this Web site?

-
-
-
-
-

11

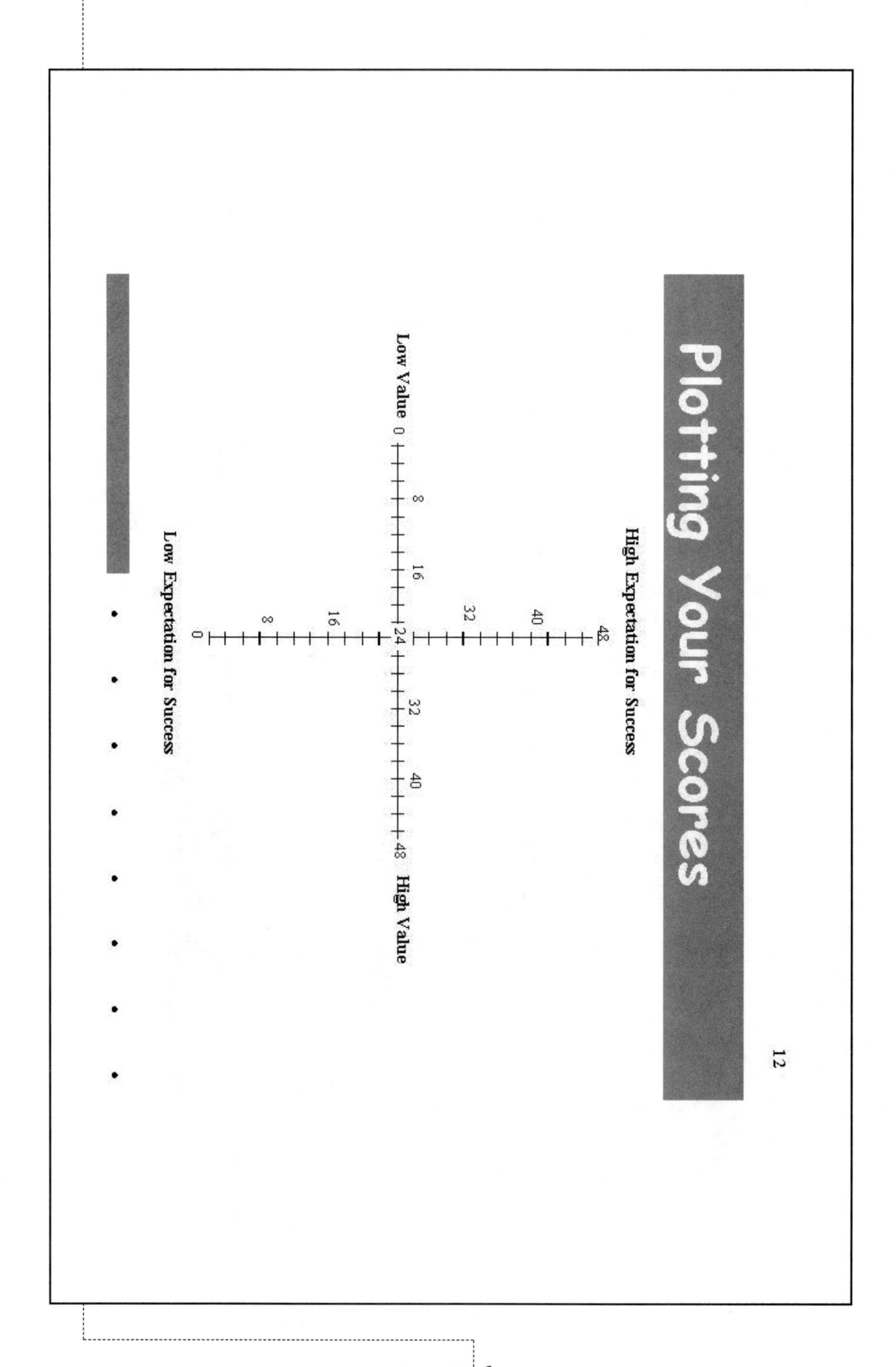

Plotting Your Scores

High Expectation for Success

Low Value 0
8
16
24
32
40
48 High Value

0 8 16 24 32 40 48

Low Expectation for Success

-
-
-
-
-
-

12

Plotting Your Scores

Average to high for Expectation for Success/
Below average to low for Value

Average to high for Value/
Average to high for Expectation for Success

Awesome Web Site!

Below average to low for Value/
Below average to low for Expectation for Success

Average to high for Value/
Below average to low for Expectation for Success

-
-
-
-
-
-

13

Class Tally

Individual Totals
V Scores

1. ___ 21. ___
2. ___ 22. ___
3. ___ 23. ___
4. ___ 24. ___
5. ___ 25. ___
6. ___ 26. ___
7. ___ 27. ___
8. ___ 28. ___
9. ___ 29. ___
10. ___ 30. ___
11. ___ 31. ___
12. ___ 32. ___
13. ___ 33. ___
14. ___ 34. ___
15. ___ 35. ___
16. ___ 36. ___
17. ___ 37. ___
18. ___ 38. ___
19. ___ 39. ___
20. ___ 40. ___

TOTAL V Scores ___
Average V Score ___

Individual Totals
XS Scores

1. ___ 21. ___
2. ___ 22. ___
3. ___ 23. ___
4. ___ 24. ___
5. ___ 25. ___
6. ___ 26. ___
7. ___ 27. ___
8. ___ 28. ___
9. ___ 29. ___
10. ___ 30. ___
11. ___ 31. ___
12. ___ 32. ___
13. ___ 33. ___
14. ___ 34. ___
15. ___ 35. ___
16. ___ 36. ___
17. ___ 37. ___
18. ___ 38. ___
19. ___ 39. ___
20. ___ 40. ___

TOTAL XS Scores ___
Average XS Score ___

The "Awesome Web Site" Award (AWArd)

Would your students like to share your Awesome Web Site discoveries with other educators or students? The authors invite individual students and entire classes of students (grades 7-12) to nominate their favorite curriculum-related Web sites for the Awesome Web Site Award (AWArd). More information on the AWArd and how to submit a nomination is available on our Web site at www.MotivationMining.com.

HIGHLIGHTS of Chapter Twelve

Here are some of the key points covered in Chapter Twelve.
▶ A set of overhead transparencies and a descriptive outline were provided to supplement your lesson on Web evaluation.
▶ Students may nominate their "Awesome Web Sites" for the Awesome Web Site Award (AWArd).

MINESTORMING

You probably have a lot of ideas for teaching Web evaluation to your students. Use this page to record your ideas or additional information that you want to include that goes beyond what was provided in Chapter Twelve.

_____
_____
_____
_____
_____
_____
_____
_____
_____
_____

Bibliography

Bibliography

Dodge, Bernie. "WebQuests: A Technique for Internet-Based Learning." *Distance Educator, 1* (20). Summer 1995: 10-13.

Hackbarth, Steven. "Web-Based Learning in the Context of K-2 Schooling." In *Educational Media and Technology Yearbook, 22*, 1997: 109-31.

Ketterer, Stan."Teaching Students How to Evaluate and Use Online Resources." *Journalism & Mass Communication Exercise.* Winter 1998: 4-14.

Nielsen, Jakob. "Heuristic Evaluation." In J. Nielsen and R.L. Mack (Eds.), *Usability Inspection Methods.* New York: John Wiley & Sons, 1994.

"Schools That Are Using the Internet: Who Are They?" *Technology Connection—The Book Report—Library Talk.* [Spec. suppl.] September 1996: 10-11.

Simpson, Carol. "Harnessing Internet Resources for the Student Researcher." *Technology Connection—The Book Report—Library Talk* [Spec. suppl]. September 1996: 3, 7.

Appendices

Appendix A:
Lesson Plans

LESSON PLAN #1

Evaluating Web Sites

School: Mexico High School, Mexico, New York

Audience: 12th grade Journalism students

Instructional Team:
Michael Charbonneau, Journalism teacher
Nancy Nicholson, library media specialist

Assignment:
Evaluate quality of several newspaper Web sites.

Materials:
Web site accuracy criteria handout, *WebMAC Senior*, computer with Internet access.

Objective:
Students will be able to analyze a Web site to determine its motivational appeal.

Procedure:
1. Ask students if some Web sites are more appealing than others.
2. Ask students to list some features of Web sites that they consider memorable.
3. Ask students what things they think should be avoided in creating a Web site.
4. Instruct students to explore Web sites of *Chicago Tribune, Oswego Palladium Times, New York Times,* and *MSNBC.*
5. Ask students what they liked or didn't like about the Web sites.
6. Explain the purpose of *WebMAC* to students and review directions.
7. Have students choose one of the Web sites and evaluate it using *WebMAC Senior.*
8. Instruct students to grade the Web site using the scoring grid.
9. Allow students to "surf" for other high school newspapers Web sites.
10. Have students critique their present Web site.
11. Have students compile a list of features they liked or did not like from the Web sites that they visited.
12. Ask students to make recommendations for changes in their Web site and why the changes should be made.
13. Ask students to name important factors in evaluating a Web site

Evaluation: Completion of worksheet and participation in discussion.

LESSON PLAN #2

Evaluating Research Sources

School: Chittenango High School

Audience: 12th grade Participation in Government students

Instructional Team:

Lynne Pascale, Participation in Government teacher,
Pamela Revercomb, library media specialist, and Wendy Scalfaro, graduate student intern

Assignment:

Research paper using four different sources on a controversial social issue

Materials:

"Taking Sides," "Opposing Viewpoints" book series,
"Electric Library," *WebMAC Senior*

Objective:

Students will recognize the importance of evaluating sources and complete *WebMAC Senior*.

Procedure:

Day 1: Teacher explains importance of evaluating sources.
Introduce book series that present opposing viewpoints and how students could use them. Show opposing viewpoints with "Clinton argument," a role play staged by Lynne and Pamela to present extreme viewpoints to grab students' attention. Begin with comment about how Clinton was on TV conducting these little interpersonal chat sessions with high school students about guns in schools, feeling safe, and so on. Pamela argues that he was an admitted liar and a total pig morally and he had no business associating with high school students, much less giving them advice on how to feel safe around others. Lynne counters with how he was the president and his opinion should still be respected. Argue for a while, then just stop and tell students this is what is meant by opposing viewpoints, controversial social issues, and so forth. Demonstrate writing thesis statement (in groups or pairs)

Day 2: Continue writing thesis statement (in groups or pairs).

Work in pairs using OPAC to find books.

Day 3: Introduction "Electric Library" (Example Topic "reintroduction of wolves"), maps, pictures, TV and radio transcripts, articles

Day 4: Teach students how to use *WebMAC Senior.* Go over directions and describe future uses (college). Have them use it while doing their research.

Day 5: Show SIRS Knowledge Source (online database). Review rules for works cited. Discuss *WebMAC* results.

Evaluation: Completed Web evaluation instruments.

Appendix B:
WebMAC Middle (2.0)

(Instrument, Score Sheets, Class Tally, and Plotting Grids)

WEBSITE MOTIVATIONAL ANALYSIS CHECKLIST
WebMAC Middle© (v.2.0)

WebMAC Middle is not a test. *There are no wrong answers.* It is a way of finding out what is good about this Web site and what needs to be improved. You are the judge. After reading each statement, circle the face that best describes how you would rate this Web site.

Before using *WebMAC Middle*, it's a good idea to spend at least 20-30 minutes exploring the Web site to be evaluated in order to have some familiarity with its content and structure. You may need to go through the Web site at least once more to complete this checklist.

Rate your level of agreement with each of the 24 statements by placing the appropriate number value on the line in front of each item. If you are not sure about any item, select the best response you can give.

> **3** = I definitely agree.
> **2** = I mostly agree.
> **1** = I somewhat agree.
> **0** = I do NOT agree

Example of completed item:
-3- 0. This Web site makes me happy.

Read each question carefully. Think about your experience with this Web site before answering each question. If you need more help understanding how to use *WebMAC Middle*, ask your teacher for help.

Name_____ URL_____

WEBMAC MIDDLE (2.0)

3 = I definitely agree.
2 = I mostly agree.
1 = I somewhat agree.
0 = I do NOT agree

_____ 1. I like the colors and backgrounds used at this Web site.

_____ 2. This Web site is well-organized.

_____ 3. The information at this Web site is accurate and unbiased.

_____ 4. All the buttons and other mechanisms for moving around in this Web site work the way they should.

_____ 5. Something (such as a picture or title) on the home page of this Web site caught my attention.

_____ 6. I can read and understand most or all of the words at this Web site.

_____ 7. This Web site has connections (links) to other interesting or useful Web sites.

_____ 8. If I get lost or need help at this Web site, there are ways of getting help.

_____ 9. This Web site is fun and interesting to explore.

_____ 10. There is a menu or site map that helps me understand how much and what kinds of information I will find there.

_____ 11. All information at this Web site is related to the main topic.

_____ 12. I can control how fast I move through this Web site at all times.

_____ 13. There are surprising or unusual things at this Web site.

_____ 14. The purpose of this Web site is clear to me.

_____ 15. I find the information contained in this Web site to be current and up-to-date.

_____ 16. I do not need any special skills or experience to use this Web site.

_____ 17. The variety of formats (e.g., text, images, sound) keeps my attention.

WEBMAC MIDDLE (2.0)

3 = I definitely agree.
2 = I mostly agree.
1 = I somewhat agree.
0 = I do NOT agree

_____ 18. No matter where I am at this Web site I can return to the home page or exit.

_____ 19. The information at this Web site is useful to me.

_____ 20. All of the Web site's links work the way they should.

_____ 21. This Web site has unusual or unique features that make it more interesting.

_____ 22. There is enough of what I am interested in (or looking for) on this Web site.

_____ 23. There is a way to communicate with the author of this Web site.

_____ 24. At all times, I can control what information at this Web site I wish to see.

Now, you are ready to answer the final questions.

This is a Web site I would like to visit again at another time.   YES ☐   No ☐

This is a Web site that friends my age would like to visit.   YES ☐   No ☐

Based on your experience with this Web site, please write below what you think are the best things about it. Then, write what you think could be improved about this Web site.

"Best Things About This Web site"

a.) _____

b.) _____

c.) _____

WEBMAC MIDDLE (2.0)

"Things That Need Improvement"

a.) _____

b.) _____

c.) _____

Overall, would you give this Web site a **thumbs up** or a **thumbs down**? Circle your answer. (If you just can't make up your mind, then circle the person who is scratching his head.)

| Gets my vote! | Undecided | Needs lots of improvement! |

Wait for instructions from your teacher or library media specialist before scoring.

SCORING WebMAC MIDDLE (2.0)

After listening to the directions, place your score for each question next to the number of that question. Notice that odd-numbered items are written under column **A** and even-numbered items are written under column **B**.

A	**B**
1. _____	2. _____
3. _____	4. _____
5. _____	6. _____
7. _____	8. _____
9. _____	10. _____
11. _____	12. _____
13. _____	14. _____
15. _____	16. _____
17. _____	18. _____
19. _____	20. _____
21. _____	22. _____
23. _____	24. _____

TOTAL
A Scores _____

TOTAL
B Scores _____

UNDERSTANDING YOUR SCORES

The "<u>A</u>" score represents how interesting or useful you feel this Web site is. A low score indicates that you don't feel it has much to offer to you personally. The "<u>B</u>" score refers to how well the Web site works. This covers things like how easy or difficult it was to find your way around, how well the designer did his or her job of making sure everything works correctly, and how clear and organized the information was. A low score here, for example, means that you did not feel confident that you could easily find your way around or get the information you needed. Once you have scored *WebMAC Middle,* you can refer to the score key below to see how well the Web site rated. A Web site that gets high scores in both <u>A</u> and <u>B</u> is an ***Awesome Web Site***!

SCORE KEY

<u>A</u> *(How Interesting)*
- 0 – 9 Poor
- 10 – 17 Below Average
- 18 – 24 Average
- 25 – 30 Good
- 31 – 36 Outstanding

<u>B</u> *(How Well It Worked)*
- 0 – 9 Poor
- 10 – 17 Below Average
- 18 – 24 Average
- 25 – 30 Good
- 31 – 36 Outstanding

Outstanding <u>A</u> + Outstanding <u>B</u> = ***Awesome Web Site!***

RATING THIS WEB SITE: INDIVIDUAL

DIRECTIONS: On the grid below, you will notice that the horizontal line is for the "How Interesting" score (the **A** score) dot for the **A** score along the *Not Interesting – Very Interesting* line; place a dot for the **B** score along the *Works Well – Works Poorly* line. Then, draw straight lines to their point of intersection. A good Web sites will have both scores in the upper right section. An awesome Web site will have scores that fall in the extreme upper right section.

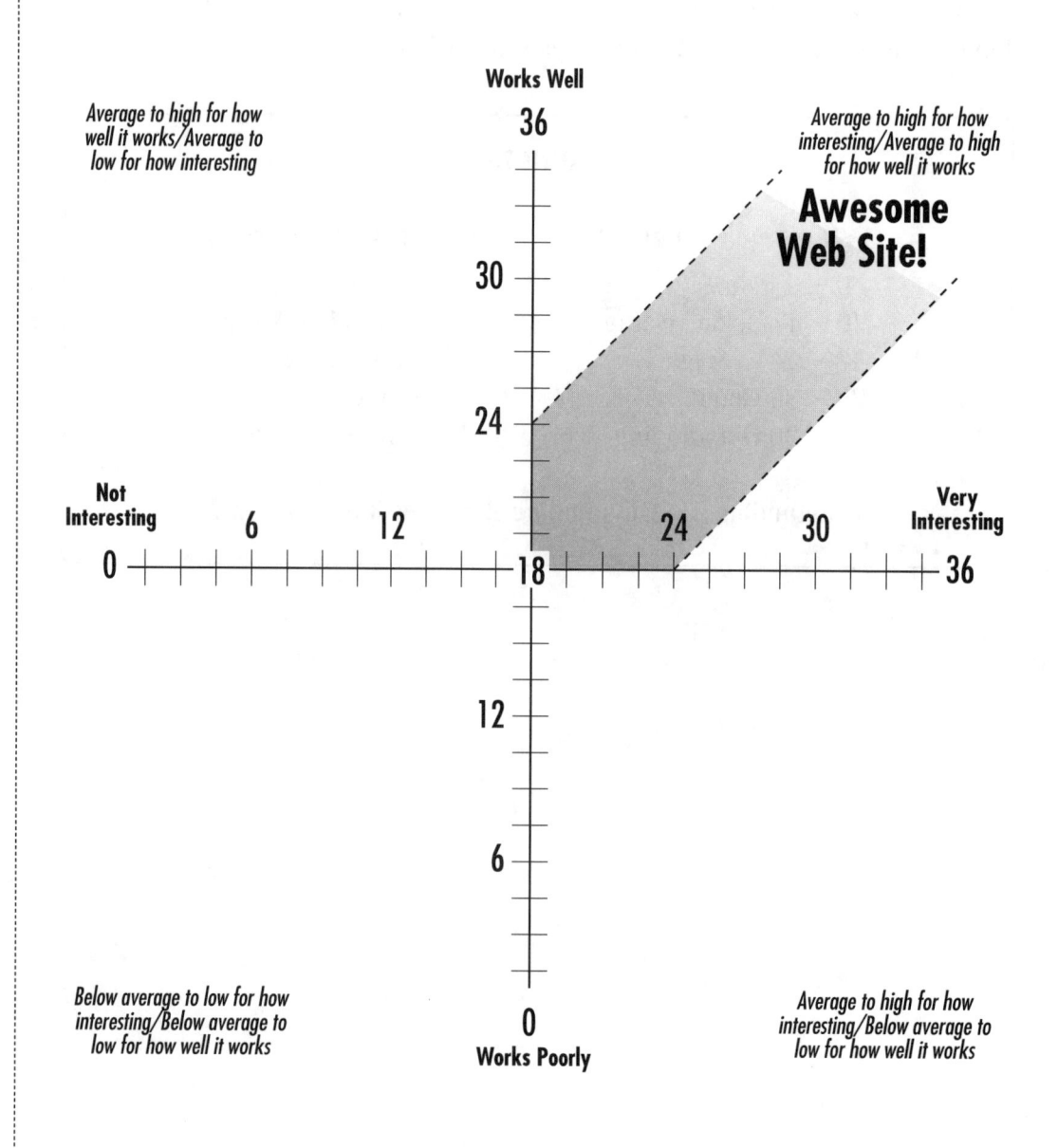

Average to high for how well it works/Average to low for how interesting

Works Well — 36

Average to high for how interesting/Average to high for how well it works

Awesome Web Site!

Not Interesting 0 — 6 — 12 — 18 — 24 — 30 — 36 **Very Interesting**

Below average to low for how interesting/Below average to low for how well it works

Works Poorly — 0

Average to high for how interesting/Below average to low for how well it works

WWW MOTIVATION MINING: FINDING TREASURES FOR TEACHING EVALUATION SKILLS, GRADES 7-12 — APPENDICES

CLASS TALLY

Use the results of the class tally sheet and plot the average **A** score (Value or *How Interesting*) and **B** score (Expectation for Success or *How Well It Works*) on the grid below.

Individual Totals		**Individual Totals**	
A Scores		**B Scores**	
1. _____	21. _____	1. _____	21. _____
2. _____	22. _____	2. _____	22. _____
3. _____	23. _____	3. _____	23. _____
4. _____	24. _____	4. _____	24. _____
5. _____	25. _____	5. _____	25. _____
6. _____	26. _____	6. _____	26. _____
7. _____	27. _____	7. _____	27. _____
8. _____	28. _____	8. _____	28. _____
9. _____	29. _____	9. _____	29. _____
10. _____	30. _____	10. _____	30. _____
11. _____	31. _____	11. _____	31. _____
12. _____	32. _____	12. _____	32. _____
13. _____	33. _____	13. _____	33. _____
14. _____	34. _____	14. _____	34. _____
15. _____	35. _____	15. _____	35. _____
16. _____	36. _____	16. _____	36. _____
17. _____	37. _____	17. _____	37. _____
18. _____	38. _____	18. _____	38. _____
19. _____	39. _____	19. _____	39. _____
20. _____	40. _____	20. _____	40. _____

Total A Scores: _____   **Total B Scores:** _____

Average A Scores: _____   **Average B Scores:** _____

RATING THIS WEB SITE: CLASS

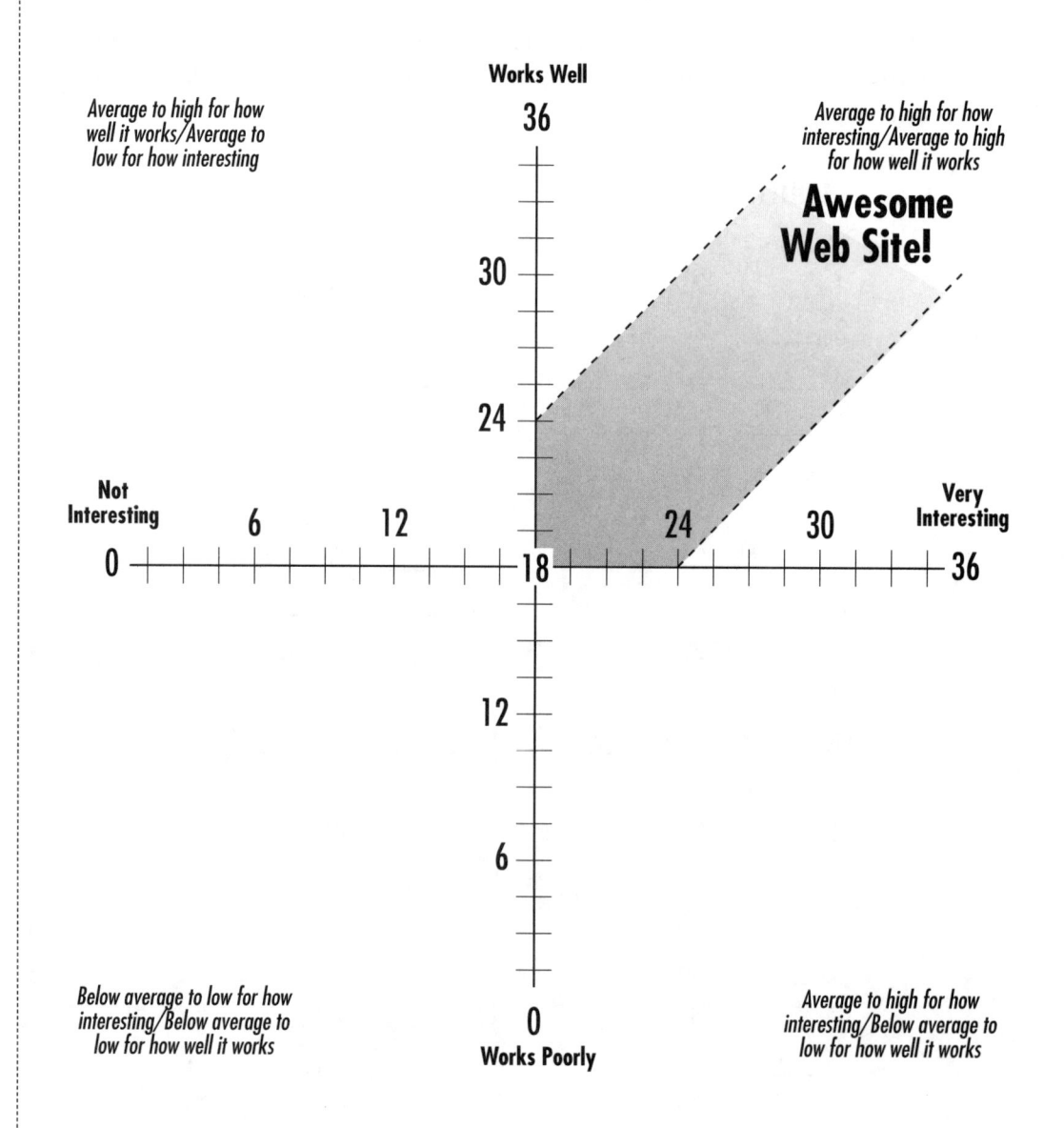

Works Well (vertical axis, 0 to 36, with "Works Poorly" at 0)
Not Interesting to **Very Interesting** (horizontal axis, 0 to 36)

Average to high for how well it works/Average to low for how interesting (upper left)

Average to high for how interesting/Average to high for how well it works (upper right)

Awesome Web Site!

Below average to low for how interesting/Below average to low for how well it works (lower left)

Average to high for how interesting/Below average to low for how well it works (lower right)

WWW Motivation Mining: Finding Treasures for Teaching Evaluation Skills, Grades 7-12 | 182 | Appendices

Appendix C:
Content Validity Checklist

CONTENT VALIDITY CHECKLIST (Arnone & Small, 1999)

The Content Validity Checklist was designed as a Web-aid for teachers screening Web sites for inclusion in lesson plans. This checklist focuses on content validity only. There are no questions about functionality, amount of information, appeal of visuals, or navigation issues since these are included in the *WebMAC* instruments. For content validity to be high, all boxes should be checked "Yes," unless an item is not applicable to your situation.

1. The source of information for this Web site is credible.   YES ☐   No ☐

   TIP: Check the home page to determine who or what entity is responsible for the content. Is there a link to background information on the author(s) or institution? Make sure you are convinced of the legitimacy and qualifications of the author.

2. There is a way to contact the author of the Web site, if necessary.   YES ☐   No ☐

3. The factual information or content of the Web site seems accurate.   YES ☐   No ☐

   TIP: Look for the sources of information. They should be clearly identified and easily verifiable. Links to other Web sites with related information may also help with verification

4. If the Web site presents concepts or principles in its domain (e.g., science, art), they are appropriately presented without confusing or missing information.   YES ☐   No ☐

   TIP: Think of your target audience. Is there enough baseline information presented to support the presentation of higher order concepts or principles?

5. There are no typographical or spelling errors that could potentially cause the information at this Web site to be misunderstood.   YES ☐   No ☐

6. The content is appropriate for your students' developmental level?   YES ☐   No ☐

7. The links from this site appear to be credible.   YES ☐   No ☐

8. This Web site appears to be free of bias.   YES ☐   No ☐

   TIP: Is there a reason the author of this Web site might be biased in the presentation of content? (For example, does the author have a vested interest in how you react

to the information provided?) Does the author identify
when a statement is a personal point of view?

9. The information on this Web site is current   YES ☐   No ☐
   enough for your needs.

   TIP Look for a "Last Update" usually located at the header or footer of a page. Often, some parts of the site will be updated regularly, while others remain fairly constant. Determine how important currency is to the presentation of your specific topic.

10. The links from this Web site are also current and unbiased.   YES ☐   No ☐

Index

Index

A
accuracy of information, 21, 184.
ARCS Model of Motivational Design, 18.
Ask-an-Expert services, 7-8.
authenticity of information, 19-20, 24, 184-85.
authority of Web site, 33, 184.
Awesome Web Site Award (AWArd), 74-75, 162.

B
bias, 21, 184-85.
Big6 Model of Information Problem-Solving, 4, 6.

C
clarity of Web site, 10.
comprehensive coverage, 21, 184.
content validity, 19-20, 21, 32-33, 124, 184-85.
Critical Evaluation Survey, 33.
currency, 21, 33, 185.
Cyberguides, 33.

D
digital literacy, 9.

E
ease of use attribute, See motivation attributes.
educational standards, 98, 5.
enthusiasm of instructor, 20, 46.
evaluation, *See* Web site evaluation.
Expectancy-Value (E-V) Theory, 17-19, 117, 122-23, 138;
    applying to Web sites, 18-23, 24-25, 60, 139-40;
    and *WebMAC*, 25, 27, 34, 117-18, 133.
expectation for success, 17-19, 22, 25, 34-35, 36, 46, 61-62, 70-71, 72-73, 123, 126-27, 131, 140.

F
FLIP-IT! Model, 4.
functionality of Web site, 21-23, 34-35.

I
information literacy, 4-6, 9-10, 13, 85, 108.
Information Power: Building Partnerships for Learning, 5.
integration with curriculum, 82-83, 92.
Internet, 6, 13, 44;
    basic terminology, 44-45, 147, 151;
    use as teaching tool, 6-9, 16.
intrinsic motivation, 16-17.

L
Library Selection Criteria for WWW Resources, 32.

M
meaningfulness attribute, See motivation attributes.
Model of the Search Process, 4.
motivation, 16-19;
    attributes, 24-25, 60-61, 70, 117, 128-31, 156-58;
    importance of, 16-17, 19, 21-23;
    See also Expectancy-Value (E-V) Theory.
motivation mining, 19, 24, 27, 117, 120-21.
motivational quality of Web sites, 20-23, 33, 61, 72-73, 117, 125-28, 139;
    See also Web site evaluation.

O
organized attribute, *See* motivation attributes.
overheads for use with *WebMAC Senior*, 119-36, 149-61.

P
Pathways to Knowledge: Follett Information Skills Model, 4, 6.

R

research models, 4, 6.
Research Process Model, 4.

S

stimulating attribute, *See* motivation attributes.
student perceptions, 19, 20-21, 125;
    See also TSA Model for Web-Based Instruction.

T

Taxonomy of Educational Objectives, 5.
teacher judgements, 19-20, 24, 124;
    See also TSA Model for Web-Based Instruction.
terminology, Internet, 44-45, 147, 151.
Thinking Critically About World Wide Web Resources, 33.
tools for Web evaluation, 20, 32-37, 132;
    See also specific tools.
TSA Model for Web-Based Instruction, 23-25, 124-25, 138-39;
    See also student perceptions;
    teacher judgements;
    Web site motivational attributes.

V

value, 17-19, 21, 24, 34, 36, 61-62, 70, 72-73, 123, 126-27, 129-30, 139.

W

Web resources:
    examples, 7-9;
    See also Web site evaluation.
Web site design, 33, 71-72, 83, 84, 102-103.
Web site evaluation, 5-6, 9-10, 17, 32-37, 44, 83-84, 146-47, 150.
Web Site Investigator, 35.
Web Site Motivational Analysis Checklist (WebMAC), 34, 133, 140;
    development of, 37;
    as lesson planning tool, 39, 97-99, 134, 140;
    other instruments, 35-37, 118;
    as research and development tool, 39-40, 71-72, 83, 84-85, 96, 99-103, 134, 140;
    as teaching tool, 38, 134, 140, 170-72;
    See also WebMAC Junior;
    WebMAC Middle;
    WebMAC Senior.
Web site motivational attributes, 19, 21-25.
WebMAC Junior, 35-36, 133.
WebMAC Middle, 36, 133, 174-182;
    administration of, 45;
    uses of, 86-87, 104.
WebMAC Senior, 35, 53-55, 133, 152;
    administration of, 45-47, 52;
    interpretation of, 70-74;
    lesson plans, 170-172;
    scoring, 60-65, 154-61;
    See also motivation attributes;
    uses of, 83-85, 87-92, 96-104, 118, 170-172;
    workshops, 116-41, 146-62.
www.MotivationMining.com, 88, 104, 109, 162.